On Histo...

Se...

by the same author

FICTION
The Shadow of the Sun
The Game
The Virgin in the Garden
Still Life
Sugar and Other Stories
Possession: A Romance
Angels and Insects
The Matisse Stories
The Djinn in the Nightingale's Eye
Babel Tower
Elementals
The Biographer's Tale

CRITICISM
Degrees of Freedom: The Novels of Iris Murdoch
Unruly Times: Wordsworth and Coleridge
Passions of the Mind: Selected Writings
Imagining Characters (with Ignês Sodré)

On Histories and Stories

Selected Essays

A. S. BYATT

Chatto & Windus

LONDON

First published 2000

1 3 5 7 9 10 8 6 4 2

© A. S. Byatt 2000

A. S. Byatt has asserted her right
under the Copyright, Designs and Patents Act 1988
to be identified as the author of this work

First published in the United Kingdom in 2000 by Chatto & Windus
Random House, 20 Vauxhall Bridge Road, London SW1V 2SA

Random House Australia (Pty) Limited
20 Alfred Street, Milsons Point, Sydney,
New South Wales 2061, Australia

Random House New Zealand Limited
18 Poland Road, Glenfield,
Auckland 10, New Zealand

Random House South Africa (Pty) Limited
Endulini, 5A Jubilee Road, Parktown 2193, South Africa

Random House UK Limited Reg. No. 954009

A CIP catalogue record for this book is available from the British Library

Papers used by Random House UK Limited are natural,
recyclable products made from wood grown in sustainable forests.
The manufacturing processes conform to the environmental
regulations of the country of origin.

ISBN 0 7011 6946 X

Typeset by SX Composing DTP, Rayleigh, Essex
Printed and bound in Great Britain
by Mackays of Chatham PLC, Chatham, Kent

For Ron and Keith Schuchard

Contents

On Histories and Stories

Selected Essays

Introduction

These essays are about the complicated relations between reading, writing, and the professional and institutional study of literature. They are a writer's essays. I am a writer, and have always seen myself primarily as a writer, though I taught English and American Literature full-time in University College London, between 1972 and 1984, and have taught literature at various times to adult classes and to art students. I have never taught 'creative writing'. I think I see teaching good reading as the best way of encouraging, and making possible, good writing.

I was honoured and happy when Professor Schuchard at Emory University invited me to give the Richard Ellmann memorial lectures. Richard Ellmann was a great and generous critic, and Professor Schuchard made it clear in his invitation that the lectures were designed to keep alive a tradition of good criticism in language available to the common reader as well as to the professional academic. Professor Peter Brooks at Yale invited me at the same time to give the Finzi-Contini lecture there. The Finzi-Contini lecture is designed to explore the relations between English-language literatures and European literatures. This invitation too excited me, since I see myself increasingly as a European writer, and have become more and more interested in contemporary European writing. I saw the three Emory lectures and the Yale lecture as an opportunity to think on a broad front about what was going on in contemporary writing, British and European.

The formal study of writing by living authors is a very recent phenomenon, which has exploded during my writing life. The study of English literature itself is less than a century old. My mother studied English in its early days at Cambridge under I.A. Richards and F.R. Leavis, who was certainly the most powerful force in the Cambridge English of my own time. In those days, although in Cambridge we read T.S. Eliot and D.H. Lawrence, the Oxford English course stopped at 1830, under the philological influence of Tolkien and C.S. Lewis. Now not only university students but schoolchildren are taught and examined on the work of living writers. Many other writers, like myself, feel very ambivalent about this. To be part of a syllabus, to be required reading, to be carefully read and discussed ensures that one's books remain in print, and have a life of their own. But the study of living writers has coincided with intense politicised fervours of various kinds in the academic community. Novels are taught if they appear to have something to contribute to the debate about 'women's writing' or 'feminism' or 'post-colonial studies' or 'postmodernism'. All this is lively and stimulating and interesting. But, as George Steiner wisely pointed out, making syllabuses, which is a political activity, is different from making a canon. A canon (which is not immutable) is (I think) what other writers have wanted to keep alive, to go on reading, over time. There is always a fear that good books may slip through the net of syllabuses, or disappear when political priorities change. Or never get noticed at all.

When I left university there were, I think, two books on contemporary British fiction, both of which concentrated on novels which reported on the class struggle, social change, and the provinces. (William Cooper, John Wain, C.P. Snow, Alan Sillitoe, David Storey.) Those of us who taught evening classes started out at least with those books. I remember meeting an older lecturer in the City Literary Institute and asking him what he was teaching. He said he was teaching Sybille Bedford's *A Legacy*. I had never heard of it. He said I wouldn't have. It didn't fit any syllabus. It was simply a masterpiece, idiosyncratic – and as it happens, historical and European. I read it and saw he was right. Equally, I was then teaching David Storey's *Radcliffe*, which superficially fitted the paradigm of class struggle in the provinces. That too is a masterpiece, a fierce, terrible, violent European masterpiece, whose debts to *Madame Bovary* and *The Idiot* are

2

more startling and extraordinary than its debts to Emily Brontë. I don't meet many people now who have read it. Its paradigm has been replaced by others, and by a new wave of assertions that English literature never reports on the provinces, is purely metropolitan. (This is a phenomenon I don't understand – the 1950s novelists did nothing that had not already and more profoundly been done by D.H. Lawrence and Arnold Bennett. Who in turn learned from George Eliot, the Brontës and Elizabeth Gaskell.)

I think those of us who write about modern writing have a duty to keep the discussion open and fluent and very broad-based. We need to create new paradigms, which will bring new books, new styles, new preoccupations to the attention of readers. We don't know what novels of this year, or last, or of ten years ago, will be being read in fifty years – if any of them will. We need to keep thinking of new – even deliberately provisional – ways to read and to compare what we have read.

My Richard Ellmann lectures are about British – largely English – novels about history. Wherever I go in Europe, as well as in Britain, there are seminars on post-colonial writing where Salman Rushdie's wit about the Empire Writing Back is quoted, and his assertion that British writing before the Empire Wrote Back was moribund and that contemporary British writing is desperately in need of enlivening, is accepted without question. The Irish have their own debate about whether Irish writing can be assimilated to post-colonial writing. They are better Europeans than the English, and they argue beautifully and passionately. They, too, are happy to suppose that English writing can be dismissed. I think that a body of writing that included Burgess, Golding, Murdoch, and Lessing, to start with, carries weight. My paradigm is designed to complicate the discussion a little. Writers are writing historical novels, but much of the discussion of *why* they are doing this has been confined within the discussions of Empire or Women, or to the debate between 'escapism' and 'relevance'. It's not so simple, as I hope I've shown. And I hope I've also managed to make a new map – not a completely new map, of course – of recent British writing, with perhaps Anthony Burgess and Penelope Fitzgerald, William Golding, Muriel Spark and Lawrence Norfolk at the centre instead of some of the others. I've written about Martin Amis and Julian Barnes, but I've also talked about John Fuller and Robert Irwin, writers hard to fit into existing paradigms, but wonderful to read.

There is a long list of writers I greatly admire and should ideally have written about as well – from J.G. Ballard whose grand *The Empire of the Sun* is an essential part of the fictive reconstruction of the lived history of the second world war, to Tibor Fischer's reconstruction of the Communist Hungary of his parents' generation in *Under The Frog* which makes an interesting comparison with the wartime stories of the Barnes-Swift generation. I might have needed a whole chapter on the profound and complex fables of Kazuo Ishiguro about the confusions and reconstructions of the post-war world, starting in Japan, and moving, book by book from Britain and Germany in *The Remains of the Day* to central Europe in *The Unconsoled* and Shanghai and the Far East in *When We were Orphans*. Fischer and Ishiguro can look at British life from inside and outside, and are different from both the post-colonial and the purely 'British' writers.

Penelope Fitzgerald's novels have turned out to be central to all my themes. The story of her reputation is particularly illuminating. For a long time it was kept alive by the passionate admiration of other writers. In academic summaries of the state of modern British fiction she appeared uneasily in lists of secondary women. The French know everything about Barbara Pym, whose English quaintness responds to their stereotypes of Englishness, but Fitzgerald's far more ambitious, far wiser, far more complex novels are ignored in their discussions of cross-Channel writing.

'Old Tales, New Forms' springs from a writerly preoccupation I turned into a scholarly one. I found myself wanting to write tales and stories, having described myself in my early days as a 'self-conscious realist', and slowly came to see that the alternative tradition of the literary tale, or fairy tale, and the related anecdote was one of the things that made it possible to talk meaningfully about European literature, as opposed to national literatures. It is a historical pre-occupation – Homer and Ovid and Norse myth are still living forces in much of Europe – and it is very modern, as works like Magris's magnificent *Danube* weave together history, geography, folklore, natural history, anecdote and myth. I rediscovered the European literary tale, going back to Goethe, Hoffman and Hans Andersen, and the new versions, at once archaic and postmodern, of Karen Blixen and Italo Calvino. My essay on the *Thousand and One Nights* for the *New York Times*'s millennial issue fitted nicely into this research – and this delicious reading – and I have included it, with its extra-European elements. I have also included a personal essay I was asked to write by Kate Bernheimer for *Mirror Mirror on the Wall* (Anchor Books, 1998) in which women writers explored their favourite fairy tales. I chose the imagery of fire, ice and mirrors, and that seems to sit happily next to Scheherazade.

'True Stories and the Facts in Fiction' was originally given as a paper at All Souls College in Oxford, as part of a series arranged by the historian Scott Mandelbrote on the writing of history. I was preoccupied with the writing of the two novellas in *Angels and Insects*, which I had just finished. These tales grew out of the literature I had been teaching at University College, and involved a great deal of historical research. I was also preoccupied with the encroachments being made by literary criticism into the forms of creative writing – such as fantasy dialogues in biographies, or complicated puns as a required part of a critical style. At the same time I thought I discerned an impossible desire for scholarly exactness in good fiction writers – like dancers changing places in an eighteenth-century dance. My essay is a personal essay about exactness and invention, the borderlines between fiction and history, and the relations of both to criticism.

I should finally like to say something about the style of these essays. I quote extensively and at length. I tell the stories of books, I describe plots. When I first studied English, extensive quotation was a necessary part of the work of the critic. I.A. Richards showed his students that they were not really reading the words as they were written. He diagnosed and exposed stock responses. And whatever Leavis's faults of dogmatic dismissal, irascibility or prescriptiveness, he was a quoter of genius, and I increasingly look on my early reading of – and reading around, and following up of – those quotations as the guarantee, the proof, that we were all indeed engaged in the common pursuit of true judgment. The criticism we studied in those early days was still predominantly the criticism of practising *writers*, demonstrating their delight in their craft, and in the craft of their predecessors. The paper I studied for at Cambridge on the history and theory of criticism allowed me to concentrate on writers thinking about the forms they used, and the nature of good writing – Henry James, Coleridge, T.S. Eliot, Arnold and his touchstones. It was a form of civilised discourse and communication between readers and writers.

Two things have happened since then. One is that so much study has been done that readers of criticism tend to see quotation as merely the good student proving that he or she has read the text in question. The other is literary theory. Most critical texts nowadays are full of quotations, but not from poems or novels. They are from critical authorities, theorists, Freud, Marx, Derrida, Foucault. All this is exciting, too. But it has led critics and theorists to make writers fit into the boxes and nets of theoretical quotations which, a writer must feel, excite most of them at present much more than literature does. Frank Kermode is not alone in deprecating the disappearance of a taste for poetry. Many writers, and some critics, feel that powerful figures in the modern critical movements feel almost a gladiatorial antagonism to the author and the authority the author claims. I think this has led to a new energy and playfulness in writers. My generation were oppressed, as well as encouraged, in their early days by the moral expectations and moral authority of Leavis or Trilling. I think many younger ones feel no relation at all to the world of academic criticism, which has moved far away from their concerns. This distance can be experienced as a space of freedom. And, more than that, an opportunity to re-establish relations with readers at large, who are spending more and more time discussing books – all sorts of books – in the vulgar tongues and frank language of every day, in book clubs. Or writing messages to the Internet and reviews on Internet bookshop pages.

I have always known that a wise writer should understand that all readers skip, and will skip. I think, unfortunately, most readers skip most quotations these days, thinking wrongly that they know them, or ought to, already. It isn't so. Good writing is always new. My quotations are like the slides in an art historical lecture – they are the Thing Itself, which is in danger of being crushed under a weight of commentary. Criticism has become a power game – I like the old forms, where the writers criticised had space to be read, not paraphrased.

It was therefore unfortunate to discover, at a late stage, that Graham Swift refuses absolutely to grant permission for quotation. This is of course his right. It has led to the loss of some elegant and subtle sentences, and some truncation and summarising, which I regret.

I am grateful to Peg Fulton, at the Harvard University Press, and to Jenny Uglow at Chatto & Windus, for the opportunity to bring together the Ellmann Lectures, the Finzi-Contini lecture, and my more personal pieces. I am also grateful for their advice and help. Gill Marsden has performed her usual magic of precision, patience, order and questioning what needed to be questioned, with a more than usually difficult agglomeration of texts and disks. The book is dedicated to Professor Schuchard, who made my visit to Emory both instructive and delightful – and bakes a pig like no one I have ever met. Also to his wife, Keith, whose Swedenborgian scholarship amazed me and whose hospitality was thoughtful and unfailing.

Fathers

During my working life as a writer, the historical novel has been frowned on, and disapproved of, both by academic critics and by reviewers. In the 1950s the word 'escapism' was enough to dismiss it, and the idea conjured up cloaks, daggers, crinolined ladies, ripped bodices, sailing ships in bloody battles. It can also be dismissed as 'pastoral'. My sister, Margaret Drabble, in an address to the American Academy of Arts and Letters, spoke out against the 'nostalgia/heritage/fancy dress/costume drama industry'. She believes passionately that it is the novelist's duty to write about the present, to confront an age which is 'ugly, incomprehensible, and subject to rapid mutations'. This is largely the position of reviewers of shortlists for literary prizes, who ask disapprovingly, 'Where are the serious depictions of the contemporary life?' These essays are not an answer to those reasonable questions, though I think it can be argued that the 'historical' novel has proved more durable, in my lifetime, than many urgent fictive confrontations of immediate contemporary reality. I think it is worth looking at the sudden flowering of the historical novel in Britain, the variety of its forms and subjects, the literary energy and real inventiveness that has gone into it. I want to ask, why has history become imaginable and important again? Why are these books *not* costume drama or nostalgia?

The renaissance of the historical novel has coincided with a complex selfconsciousness about the writing of history itself. Hayden White[1] begins his book about history and narrative with a quotation from Roland Barthes, who said that 'narrative is simply there, like life itself . . . international, transhistorical, transcultural'. White is interested in the refusal of narrative by contemporary historians, who are sensitive to the selective, ideological shapes produced by the narrator, the narrator's designs and beliefs. Historians like Simon Schama have recently made very deliberate attempts to restore narration, and a visible narrator, to history. Schama's *Dead Certainties* (*Unwarranted Speculations*) appeared after his best-selling histories of the Dutch Golden Age and the French Revolution. It was characterised as a 'novel' and was in fact a patchwork of interrelated histories – the death of James Wolfe at the battle of Quebec in 1759, and the 1849 murder in Boston of George Parkman, the historian, whose nephew was to write Wolfe's biography. In this factual fiction, which made many readers very uneasy and unsettled, Schama mixed his own inventions and speculations into the historical facts. Other writers, particularly biographers, have taken up such hybrid and selfconscious narrative devices. Peter Ackroyd, in his biography of Dickens, and D.J. Taylor in his biography of Thackeray, have inserted imaginary dialogues between subject and biographer. Richard Holmes invents a new form for each of his life-stories, beginning with the wonderful *Footsteps*, which connects Mary Wollstonecraft, Stevenson, the Shelleys and de Nerval, with tantalising and oblique revelations of Holmes's own autobiographical reasons for choosing these particular subjects to follow and imagine. My own short novel, *The Biographer's Tale*, is about these riddling links between autobiography, biography, fact and fiction (and lies). It follows a poststructuralist critic who decides to give up, and write a coherent life-story of one man, a great biographer. But all he finds are fragments of other random lives – Linnaeus, Galton, Ibsen – overlapping human stories which make up the only available tale of the biographer. It is a tale of the lives of the dead which make up the imagined worlds of the living. It is a study of the aesthetics of inventing, or re-inventing, or combining real and imaginary human beings.

Beyond the serious aesthetic and philosophical study of the forms of history in the last decade, lay a series of cultural prohibitions derived from intellectual beliefs about life as a cultural product. We cannot know the past, we are told – what we think we know is only our own projection of our own needs and preoccupations onto what we read and reconstruct. Ideology blinds. All interpretations are provisional, therefore any interpretation is as good as any other – truth is a meaningless concept, and all narratives select and distort. Hayden White is wise about the narrative energy Fredric Jameson's Marxist analysis of history derives from the narrative nature of the Marxist account of reality itself. 'The history of all hitherto existing society is the history of class struggle . . .' Jameson says. Marxism is a master narrative whose amplitude allows us to 'unite all the individual stories of societies, groups and cultures into a single great story', White comments. He quotes Jameson on modern life as 'a single great collective story . . . the collective struggle to wrest a realm of Freedom from a realm of Necessity . . . vital episodes in a single vast unfinished *plot . . .*'[2]

I think the fact that we have in some sense been forbidden to think about history is one reason why so many novelists have taken to it. The sense of a new possibility of narrative energy, as I said, is another. Recent historical novels cover almost every time, from the Neanderthal to the Second World War, from mediaeval monks to nineteenth-century scientists, from Restoration beaux to French revolutionaries. It could be argued that the novelists are trying to find historical paradigms for contemporary situations – Rose Tremain has said that she sees the England of the restoration of Charles II as an analogy for Thatcher's Britain, and novels about the French Revolution may have something to say about the revolutionary atmosphere of the 1960s. It may be argued that we cannot understand the present if we do not understand the past that preceded and produced it. This is certainly true of the war novels I shall discuss in this essay. But there are other, less solid reasons, amongst them the aesthetic need to write coloured and metaphorical language, to keep past literatures alive and singing, connecting the pleasure of writing to the pleasure of reading.

One very powerful impulse towards the writing of historical novels has been the political desire to write the histories of the marginalised, the forgotten, the unrecorded. In Britain this has included the histories of blacks and women, and the whole flourishing and brilliant culture of the post-colonial novel, from Rushdie's India and Pakistan, through Caryl Phillips's novel of slavery, *Cambridge*, and Timothy Mo's account of Hong Kong and opium, *An Insular Possession*. I am not going to discuss these novels, because they are already the subject of much scholarship, and also because I want to complicate the impression everyone has, that the main energies of modern British writing come from what the South African Christopher Hope calls 'writers from elsewhere'. I think the existence of these often polemical revisionist tales has given other British writers the impulse to range further historically and geographically than the immediately post-war social realists. But I also think that exciting things were going on anyway, in the work of Anthony Burgess, William Golding, and others, who were neither moribund nor insular.

This first essay is about narratives of war, or about war. I became interested in this subject partly because I became interested in the slippage between personal histories and social or national histories. I began to write a novel called *The Virgin in the Garden* in the 1960s. Part of the impulse behind it was that I felt that I had now lived long enough to have lived in something I experienced as 'history', and this was a great relief to me, as I didn't want to write personal novels about the constitution of the Self, and yet as a beginning novelist I had no other subject-matter I could claim. I was born in 1936, and lived through the war and its aftermath, though hardly conscious of much of it. My novel was about what was called the new Elizabethan Age, and carried with it the ghost of the first Elizabethan Age, with its English literature of the Golden Age. Part III of the projected quartet of which that novel, with its images of history was the first, appeared only in 1996 although it was set in 1968, which meant that I was doing historical research on things I had in some sense lived through. And this sense of the edge between lived and imagined history made me in turn interested in a group of novels by young men – Graham Swift, Julian Barnes, Ian McEwan, Martin Amis – about the war they were too young to have experienced, their fathers' war. I was interested in images they had fabricated that didn't quite ring true in my experience (but I was a small child, then). I was interested in how their selection of subject-matter did and didn't coincide with that of the older generation who had lived and fought in the war, my own father's generation, Henry Green, Evelyn Waugh, Burgess, Golding. I was interested in narratives written during that historical cataclysm when its end was not known, histories without hindsight or foresight.

For me the great recorders of the immediate feel of the war were those late modernists, Henry Green and Elizabeth Bowen. The American war was soldiers going out and facing death in remote places. The European war was countries overrun and huge movements of desperate populations. The British war was a peculiar mixture of social upheaval, insular solidarity, and death from the air. As a child I remember parents and teachers expressing a curious emotion of guilt at their aesthetic excitement over the beauty of the flames and the searchlights of the Blitz. The luridly lit, hallucinatory landscape of burning London went in the novels with themes of uncertain identity, treachery, unfaithfulness and some essential instability of the Self. The hero of Green's *Caught*[3], Richard Roe, is, as the novelist was, an upper-class volunteer to the auxiliary fire service during the phoney war. His son has been abducted by the mad sister of the station chief, Pye, who is trying to keep himself unconscious of her madness and of its possible root in a possible incestuous encounter. Roe is caught in a socially fluid situation where the auxiliaries suck up to the professionals and class counts for nothing. He cannot explain himself to his sister-in-law, Di.

'The first night,' he said, 'we were ordered to the docks. As we came over Westminster Bridge it was fantastic, the whole of the left side of London seemed to be alight.'

(It had not been like that at all. As they went, not hurrying, but steadily towards the river, the sky in that quarter, which happened to be the east, beginning at the bottom of streets until it spread over the nearest houses, was flooded in a second sunset, orange and rose, turning the pavements pink. Civilians hastened by twos and threes, hushed below the stupendous pall of defeat until, in the business quarter, the streets were deserted.)

(These firemen at last drove out onto the bridge. Here, two men and a girl, like grey cartridge paper under this light which stretched with the spread of a fan up the vertical sky, were creeping off drunkenly, defiantly singing.)

(The firemen saw each other's faces. They saw the water below a dirty yellow towards the fire; the wharves on that far side low and black, those on the bank they were leaving a pretty rose. They saw the whole fury of that conflagration in which they had to play a part. They sat very still, beneath the immensity. For, against it, warehouses, small towers, puny steeples seemed alive with sparks from the mile high pandemonium of flame reflected in the quaking sky. This fan, a roaring red gold, pulsed rose at the outside edge, the perimeter round which the heavens, set with stars before fading into utter blackness, were for a space a trembling green.)

'I almost wetted my trousers,' he said, putting into polite language the phrase current at his substation.

'I had an old crook called Arthur Piper on my crew that first evening,' he went on, 'he was killed about three hours after . . . When he saw the blaze from the bridge all he said was 'Oh, mother.' . . .

'Don't talk about people being killed.'

'Well, he was.'

The gap between the Miltonic grandeur of the blaze, (which Green gives in brackets) and what Di perceives as a very dull description, is part of the pattern of the book. It finds an echo in Bowen's story, 'Mysterious Kôr',[4] where moonlit London looks like 'the moon's capital – shallow, cratered, extinct', eerie because 'the sky, in whose glassiness floated no clouds but only opaque balloons, remained glassy-silent. The Germans no longer came by the full moon. Something more immaterial seemed to threaten.' In her novel, *The Heat of the Day*,[5] which she started in 1944, she describes a London full of organic power and 'phantasmagoric' traffic, 'a source from which heavy motion boiled, surged, and not to be damned up [sic], forced for itself new channels'. Sleeplessness, she says, disembodied the lookers-on.

Apathetic, the injured and dying in the hospitals watched light change on walls which might fall tonight. Those rendered homeless sat where they had been sent; or worse, with the obstinacy of animals retraced their steps to look for what was no longer there. Most of all the dead, from mortuaries, from under cataracts of rubble, made their anonymous presence – not as today's dead, but as yesterday's living – felt through London. Uncounted, they continued to move in shoals through the city day, pervading everything to be seen or heard or felt with their torn-off senses, drawing on this tomorrow they had expected – for death cannot be so sudden as that . . . The wall between the living and the living became less solid as the wall between the living and the dead thinned. In that September transparency, people became transparent, only to be located by the just darker flicker of their hearts.

In this sensuously present ghostly world, Stella, the heroine, is tormented by Harrison, a spiv, or secret agent, who tells her that her lover, Robert, is a traitor and a spy. The plot is a shadow-play, and the resolution is violent. It is interesting that at the moment when Stella and Robert are alone together, Bowen invokes History as a ghostly third at their table.

But they were not alone, nor had they been from the start, from the start of love. Their time sat in the third place at their table. They were the creatures of history, whose coming together was of a nature possible in no other day – the day was inherent in the nature. The relation of people to one another is subject to the relation of each to time, to what is happening . . . In dwelling upon the constant for our reassurance, we forget that the loves in history have been agonizingly modern loves in their day. War at present worked as a thinning of the membrane between the this and the that, it was a becoming apparent – but then what else is love?

War has caused the lovers' – and the author's – view of time to become determinist. History is hypostasised as an entity, like war, and like love. And later, when Robert reveals his inadequate reasons for his treachery, that too is part of a dreamily determined drift. Stella asks him whether he wants the enemy to win because he believes in revolution, or because he has ceased to believe in revolution as progress, 'so that now revolution coming could only be the greatest convulsion so far, with the least meaning of all?"* He can only answer fatalistically that 'this war's just so much bloody quibbling about something that's predecided itself. Either side's winning would stop the war. Only their side's winning would stop the quibbling.' Bowen has shown us the roots of Robert's secretiveness and revolt in his dreary, loveless family in their gloomy 'Holmdene' in Sussex. They are a deadly England that is being burned and melted in the firestorm. A character in a wartime Bowen story, 'Summer Night', sees the war as an apocalypse, after which there must be a new world and a new art. Again the glare of the conflagration is the central metaphor.

> 'Now that there's enough death to challenge being alive we're facing it that, anyhow, we don't live. We're confronted by the impossibility *of* living – unless we can break through to something else . . . We can no longer express ourselves: what we say doesn't even approximate to reality; it only approximates to what's been said. I say this war's an awful illumination; it's destroyed our dark; we have to see where we are. Immobilized, God help us, and each so far apart that we can't even try to signal to each other. And our currency's worthless – our "ideas", so on, so on. We've got to mint a new one. We've got to break through to the new form – it needs genius. We're precipitated, this moment between genius and death.'

The speaker is treated ironically, but the note of excitement, of an energy of disturbance, is part of the immediate atmosphere of the war.

I turn briefly now to the comic chronicles of the war and the interwar years, written by writers who were soldiers themselves, Evelyn Waugh and Anthony Powell. Chronicles is an apt word for the form of narrative they choose – Powell's *A Dance to the Music of Time* might almost be compared to mediaeval forms like Piers Plowman, with the fair field full of folk meeting and parting, observed for their place in the social and moral tapestry of a whole time. Both Powell and Waugh

---

* It is surprising how many characters in British wartime novels *lose* any revolutionary faith they once had. The French novel is surely different. Compare my later discussion of Golding's *Free Fall*, pp. 22–23.

observe with comic glee the way in which army life, and the upheavals in civilian society, destroyed the old social order and certainties and provided endless new 'types' to be displayed and relished with that mixture of caricature and precision which runs through English fiction from Chaucer to Dickens. Both set their deflated, mock-heroic history against older, devalued, visions of honour and courage, nation and loyalty. Waugh's Guy Crouchback[6] begins his pilgrimage in Fascist Italy, where he visits the tomb of an English Crusader, touches his sword, and asks him to 'pray for me and for our endangered kingdom'. He is driven to the station by a black-shirted taxi-driver, who pontificates about a personified History. 'History is a living force. No one can put a stop to it and say, "After this date there shall be no changes." With nations as with men, some grow old . . . But if it comes to a war everyone will have too little. *They* know that. *They* will not have a war.' But there is a war, and Crouchback's experience is both grim and farcical, soldiers are clowns or spivs, heroes are without honour and daemonic madmen sprout amongst the ranks, new forms of irresponsible life and sensibility. Crouchback's high vision of dedication to God and the kingdom seems remote and anachronistic from the start. More sympathetic, in his mixture of comedy and pathos, is Powell's Welsh bank manager turned Company Commander, Rowland Gwatkin,[7] who has, as Powell's narrator, Nick, remarks, the Christian name of a military paladin, Roland dying at Roncesvalles, and a diminutive surname meaning 'little Wat'. (Any English reader over a certain age would think of the peasant rebel leader, Wat Tyler. Gwatkin bridges a class divide, is a new class embodied.) Gwatkin cherishes a regard for Kipling's Roman Centurion, watching lonely on Hadrian's Wall, and Powell describes his aspirations in a way that rapidly, and surprisingly when one reflects on it, associates much of European literature and culture with him.

> He gave the impression of being something more than a civilian keen on his new military role, anxious to make a success of an unaccustomed job. There was an air of resolve about him, the consciousness of playing a part to which a high destiny had summoned him. I suspected he saw himself in much the same terms as those heroes of Stendhal . . . an aspiring

restless spirit, who, released at last from the cramping bonds of life in a provincial town, was about to cut a dashing military figure against a backcloth of Meissonier-like imagery of plume and breast-plate: dragoons walking their horses through the wheat, grenadiers at ease in a tavern with girls bearing flagons of wine. Esteem for the army – never, in this country regarded in the continental manner, as a popular expression of the national will – implies a kind of innocence.

Powell's conduct of his twelve-book chronicle is aesthetically very subtle, and has not, I think, been wholly appreciated by the British, who tend to despise him mildly for snobbery, or to collect his characters as choice specimens of class and manners, depending on their own social predilections. He begins his account of World War II[8] with a long passage about the narrator's childhood just before the outbreak of World War I, in a house full of 'ghosts', which both cause the comic appearance of a nude housemaid, and become identified with the Eumenides, the Furies, the Kindly Ones, who 'inflicted the vengeance of the gods by bringing in their train war, pestilence, dissension on earth; torturing too, by the stings of conscience'. Nick's father, who has already (in an earlier volume set later in time than this passage), been seen as a negotiator at the Versailles treaty which imposed the peace conditions on defeated Germany, is here seen discussing with General Conyers the coming war when 'Clausewitz's nation in arms', caught between 'the Scylla of her banking system and the Charybdis of her socialist party', will have no alternative but to attack. The schoolboy narrator chats to individual batmen and military policemen at the barracks, and thinks of G.A. Henty's adventure stories of empire. The narrative is at once mythic (the Furies), Dickensian comic (the ghosts), analytic history (Clausewitz and comparisons with the Boer War), and entirely personal – Nick, the child at the barracks, spends the end of the novel trying to get called up to fight for his country. Powell's method is to weave historical time in and out of the dance of his huge cast of fictive people, who are at once individual and typical of their class, sex and education. His narration appears to be straightforward tale-telling, but is not. One of his novels may consist of two long conversations and a series of rapid incidents joining them;

one may weave back and forth in time, like memory; anecdotes are framed, as is the anecdote of the nude housemaid, by portents of recurrent personal and national disaster. The easy resourcefulness of the inwoven range of human idiosyncrasy and cultural reference is startling when we come to the later sparse tales of the post-war generation. His world, like Bowen's and Waugh's, may be disintegrating, but it is a plenum of life and cross-referencing of thought.

After the immediate metaphor, and the considered chronicle, there are a variety of wartime tales, each with their own form. Two which might be compared are *Human Voices* by Penelope Fitzgerald and *The Girls of Slender Means* by Muriel Spark. Both have the feeling of being elegant (in the mathematical sense) moral fables constructed out of the immediate accidental stuff of wartime. Spark's novel was published in 1963 and is set in 1945. Fitzgerald's was published in 1980 and is set in the days after the evacuation of Dunkirk. Both grew out of the personal war experiences of their writers. Both are sharp social comedies with what might be thought of as a metaphysical or religious dimension. Spark's girls of slender means are the impoverished gentlewomen (also the poor in spirit, she explains, ambivalently) who inhabit the May of Teck Club, amongst the ruined buildings like decayed teeth or ancient castles. They swap clothing coupons and share a Schiaparelli dress. Joanna Childe, the vicar's daughter, teaches elocution, and Selina Redwood, slender student of deportment, is thin enough to go through the lavatory window to sunbathe nude on the roof. Joanna's fragments of great verse – Hopkins, Arnold, Coleridge, Shakespeare – punctuate the tale of pinpricks of petty treachery, sexual intrigue and greed, like a counterpoint of meaning and spiritual energy, until an unexploded bomb in the next garden destroys the house, and with it Joanna, who is too solid to escape through the window, and dies reciting 'The Wreck of the Deutschland'. Selina returns to rescue, not Joanna, but the Schiaparelli dress, giving her lover, Nick, a vision of evil which causes him to join the priesthood and to be martyred in Haiti. (Spark's fable has much in common with T.S. Eliot's play, *The Cocktail Party*.) Joanna's name, Childe, an innocent name, an epithet for heroes, connects her to Gwatkin as Roland, and to Crouchback and his crusader. Selina inherits the earth. In a one-page description of the

Victory celebrations before Buckingham Palace Nick sees a seaman silently knife a girl, and a fight between British and American servicemen.

> Two men lay unconscious at the side of the path being tended by their friends. The crowds cheered in the distance behind them. A formation of aircraft burst across the night sky. It was a glorious victory.[9]

The novel ends with the words 'long ago in 1945'. The days of the characters' youth, of the conflagration, of both faith and evil are long ago – legendary – and 1963 is the world that was made by the mixed energies evident in the activities of the crowd at the Victory celebration.

Fitzgerald's Broadcasting House has the same surreal quality as the May of Teck Club in its shelled landscape. It is compared to the *Queen Mary*, with blazing portholes blacked-out at night.

> With the best engineers in the world, and a crew varying between the intensely respectable and the barely sane, it looked ready to scorn any disaster of less than Titanic scale.[10]

Fitzgerald sees this institution in both a heroic and a ruthlessly comic light. She says, with a resonant seriousness in an ironic tone:

> Broadcasting House was in fact dedicated to the strangest project of the war, or of any war, that is, telling the truth. Without prompting the BBC had decided that truth was more important than consolation, and in the long run, would be more effective. And yet there was no guarantee of this. Truth ensures trust, but not victory, or even happiness. But the BBC had clung tenaciously to its first notion, droning quietly on, at intervals from dawn to midnight, telling, as far as possible, exactly what happened.

This is a comic and innocent heroism, like Joanna Childe's, and the cast are – varying, indeed between the intensely respectable and the barely sane – a mixture like that in the May of Teck Club, dangerous innocents, moral blackmailers and lost souls. There is the same sense of a wartime saturnalia, and the same sense of a moral or religious order, preserved and betrayed. One wonderful episode describes a disastrous broadcast by a refugee French General, who appeals to historical inevitability, entreats the British to surrender, and falls dead at the microphone. The hero is the Director of Programme Planning, a good, exhausted and reasonable man, who disconnects the microphone. Like Joanna Childe he becomes a sacrificial victim, half tragic, half comic. Both Spark's and Fitzgerald's novels end with a bomb. The one in *Human Voices* is a silent unexploded parachute bomb, resting against the kerb outside Broadcasting House.

> In size and shape it approximately resembled a taxi, and passers by in fact mentioned that they had thought it was a taxi. It was understandable therefore that DPP, who appeared anyway to have something on his mind, should walk up to it, and confusing it in the darkness, try to open what might have been, but was not, a door. Anyone might have done this, but it was tragic that it should have been an Old Servant, and within a few yards of Broadcasting House.

The examples I have given so far have been narratives which worked in and against the forms of chivalric tales, and behind those, saints' lives and the Bible. I'd like to add to these the work of Anthony Burgess, whose *Earthly Powers* (1980) is a monstrous narrative, covering two world wars, and a great deal of political, religious and literary history, in a form which could superficially be said to resemble the comic chronicles of Waugh and Powell, but is in fact very different. Burgess said that no one had understood that his novel was a parody of the blockbuster, the film epic, works like *The Godfather*. One of the interesting things about postmodern fiction is the way in which it can flickeringly and variously parody almost anything, for almost any purpose. These parodies are not necessarily satirical – more often they are simultaneously simply comic and seriously analytical. Burgess's book is a furiously religious book about the demonic aspects of the kitsch of modern politics and religion – and indeed, art. He uses, among others, the device of inserting his fictional narrator, the Coward or Maugham-like homosexual novelist and public figure, into real historical situations. His hero visits a film festival in the Third Reich, unintentionally saves Himmler's life, like Wodehouse broadcasts on behalf of the Nazis (but codes in the messages 'Fuck the bloody Nazis', and 'May Hitler rot in Hell'). Burgess writes invented hagiography, invented music-hall songs, invented newspaper reports, invented documentary into his compendious mock-epic, which is at once a deadly serious allegory about Good, Evil, and Ambiguity, and a papery farce.

Burgess, who had a Catholic upbringing and sensibility, saw life and the novel in terms of religious narrative paradigms. His modern novels are riddled with representations of the conflict between Pelagius and St Augustine about free will and determinism. In this at least he resembles William Golding, whose *Darkness Visible*, which takes its title from Milton's description of Hell, opens with a burning boy advancing out of the inferno of burning bombed London, and moves into a dark parable about the nature of the production of evil, in the days of student terrorism. Golding fought in the war, in the navy – I shall come back to *Pincher Martin*, his sea-tale, but it is interesting to compare *Free Fall* with *Earthly Powers*, as a study of freedom and determinism, of good and evil. Golding in his day was modern because he made narrative forms which related to matters more primitive and more like myths than modern realism. *Free Fall* is like a modernist *Pilgrim's Progress* in which the hero Sammy Mountjoy grows up in Paradise Hill, is the subject of a spiritual battle between a virtuous rationalist scientist and a sadistic Christian woman teacher, betrays a girl called Beatrice, and is confined by the Gestapo in a cell in the dark to be interrogated about his fellow-prisoners' escape plans. Treachery, betrayal, are a constant in plots of war novels, and Sammy fails to be heroic or faithful. But when he screams in mere terror, he has a vision of the 'shining singing cosmos' and an intuition that 'complete death must be to get out of the way of that shining, singing cosmos and let it shine and sing'. He is released by a benign and just German, who says that Dr Halde, Sammy's tormenter and interrogator, 'did not understand peoples'. He sees his fellow-prisoners as angelic beings, clothed in flame and majesty, and the essence of the world as depending on a substance which he claims had been dispensed with by 'the brilliance of our political vision and the profundity of our scientific knowledge'.

It had caught no votes, it had not been suggested as a remedy for war, it was accounted for, if any account was needed, as a byproduct of the class system, the same way you get aniline dyes from the distillation of coal – an accident almost. This substance was a kind of vital morality, not the relationship of a man to remote posterity nor even a social system, but the relation of individual man to individual man – once an irrelevance but now seen to be the forge in which all change, all value, all life is beaten out into a good or bad shape.

The urgency of Sammy's vision is endorsed and created by Golding's apocalyptic and rich descriptions of transfiguration and light. What Sammy – who is a failed 1930s communist – is advocating could be seen as old-fashioned liberal humanism, presented with evangelical fervour, and – the passage is too long for me to quote – in images alternately drawn from science (including the ideas of free fall and the conservation of energy) and visionary literature. The topos of the tortured betrayer will recur in my discussion of Graham Swift. Golding himself is a literary anomaly, who uses poetically charged, anti-realist forms to defend the liberal idea of the individual, which is increasingly brought into question in later fictions. Sammy Mountjoy is Everyman. His wartime experience contains the metaphors of blazing illumination and absolute blackout, or darkness visible, we have seen in Bowen and Green. He is, essentially, an artist. His art comes from the war. His best work derives directly from the prison camp.

> It seemed natural to me that this added perception in my dead eyes should flow over into work, into portraiture. That is why those secret, smuggled sketches of the haggard, unshaven kings of Egypt in their glory are the glory of my right hand and likely to remain so. My sketches of the transfigured camp, the prison which is no longer a prison are not so good, I think, but they have their merit. One or two of them see the place with the eye of innocence or death, see the dust and the wood and the concrete and the wire as though they had just been created. But the world of miracle I could not paint then or now.

I'd like to mention, more or less in parenthesis, to illustrate the variety of ways in which the rewriting of the war can be done, two other novels about art and war, art and death, both beautifully written and surprising. They are Peter Everett's *Matisse's War* (1997) and Robert Irwin's *Exquisite Corpse* (1995). Irwin's novel is about a member of an imaginary English surrealist brotherhood whom he follows from 1936, when it was possible to invent fantastic deaths, and stage surreal suicides in the dark, through Hitler's exhibition of degenerate Art, to wartime London, where the landscape of the Blitz provides endless surreal images.

> I left my surrealist box of tricks unopened for the remainder of the War. The Blitz provided its own Surrealist effects – a white horse galloping around inside a burning meat market and displaying all its teeth in a panicked, mirthless grin, a girl in a blue dress emerging with her skipping rope from clouds of black smoke and skipping calmly by, and the façades of buildings curving and distending like the sets of *The Cabinet of Dr Caligari*. Everywhere I walked I saw staircases which led nowhere, baths suspended in mid-air, brick waterfalls flowing out of doorways and objects jumbled incongruously together in conformity with Lautréamont's aesthetic prescription: 'Beautiful as the chance meeting of an umbrella and a sewing machine on a dissecting table.'

If the Blitz outdoes surrealism, Belsen annihilates it. Going there as a war artist (with Mervyn Peake) the narrator cannot work.

> Hitherto I had taken it for granted that art and literature covered everything in the universe, or at least they could cover everything. There were no forbidden zones. I now felt that this was not true.

Matisse's War is a brilliant intertextual retelling of the wartime experiences of Henri Matisse, trying to preserve the calm of his great painting, and of Louis Aragon, surrealist poet, communist, resistance fighter, and Aragon's mistress, Eva Triolet, novelist, unbelieving Jew, resistance fighter, post-war literary heroine. Both Everett and Irwin have an extraordinary capacity to create gripping narratives which do embody their real understanding of the urgency of the ideas of their characters, real or invented. The forms of their fictions rise out of the ideas that live in them. Everett uses Aragon's *Henri Matisse, Roman*, and his *Défense du Luxe* to counterpoint the historical horrors of wartime with Matisse's Platonic vision. Words sing against each other in the two narratives. Matisse's meanings of the words 'history' and 'freedom' are to do with Cézanne's liberation of painting from perspective, his discovery of colour. 'Those olive trees in the garden are hundreds of years old. That is history.' This statement is immediately juxtaposed with Elsa's discovery of the corpse of a woman killed by the Resistance for collaboration for spying – Everett describes the absent knickers, the torn nylons, the perfume, the wound. The two paragraphs exist together. Ghosts in Matisse's world are the vanishing furniture in the vision of the Red Studio. In Aragon's they are the Vichy Collaborators

> Ghosts, ghosts, ghosts
> Generals with no armies, Admirals with no fleet
> Well-paid to rise late, sleep early . . .
> That Vichy steakhouse, auctioning
> France's flesh, roasted or raw.

Iris Murdoch, who worked in the refugee camps after the war, took from Simone Weil the concept of Até, the automatic handing-on of pain and cruelty, and out of it created a series of wounded enchanter-figures who destroy peace-time lives in the aftermath of war. Some sense of the afterlife of damage and death-dealing informs the novels I want to turn to next, those by writers born after the war, Graham Swift, Julian Barnes, Pat Barker, Martin Amis. The difference in atmosphere between their novels and the blaze of excitement and energy of thought of the wartime writers is startling. One reason at least is that they are often quite deliberately working with clichés, with popular images of wartime derived from films they saw as boys about the bravery of Spitfire pilots and secret agents, or spies under inter-rogation. Fredric Jameson has written perceptively about 'what the French call *la mode retro*, the "nostalgia film", pastiche of popular culture within popular culture itself'.[11] Makers of films about the fifties in the seventies and eighties, he observes, are nostalgic, not for the fifties values, but for the experience they had when seeing the films as innocent audiences. These post-war English novelists use the bare clichés of war films – the Spitfire pilot coming down in flames, or alone in the clouds, the brave man cracking under interrogation, the ministries of fear and secret files. They use them quite deliberately, to write about what I think is their own sense of living in an aftermath, an unheroic time with no urgency and no images – though this is complicated by that generation's paralysing sense of the possibility of nuclear annihilation, of the wiping-out of all futures and all continuity. David Hare's 1970s play, *Plenty*, is one example of this. His central character, Susan, was a British agent helping the French resistance. Her experience of violence and extreme danger makes her unable to live in peace-time plenty; and her damaged ideals turn her into a purposeless rebel, breaking things for the sake of breaking them. Hare himself has a romantic nostalgia for an absolute faith in something, and mixes Susan's impatience with the 'revolutionary' politics of the comfortable seventies politicised intellectuals in a way I find unsatisfactory compared to, say, Everett's understanding of what Aragon was fighting for.

Much more interesting is Graham Swift's bleak and schematic little book, *Shuttlecock*, whose subtitle is 'a psychological thriller'. The hero of this is employed in a government department that investigates and deals with the records of past crimes. His office is reminiscent of those inhabited by the heroes of le Carré and Deighton, crossed with a Kafkaesque aimlessness. He begins his narration by telling how he was driven to torture his hamster; it later turns out that his sex-life consists of ever more ingenious and tortuous painful scenes. His father was dropped behind enemy lines in France as an agent, was captured and tortured and escaped. The father wrote a best-selling account of his heroism, under the title of *Shuttlecock*, which was his code-name, a figure for a man on the end of a parachute. The narrator is now obsessively reading and rereading the book. The father is speechless and motionless in a mental hospital. His breakdown may have something to do with the fact that his son's superior is investigating his files. It is possible that he did not remain heroically silent – that he betrayed his friends and collaborators. It is possible that his autobiography is a fiction, designed to impress his son. The narrator tortures, beats up, terrifies his sons, whom he accuses of stealing his father's book. Salvation comes when he decides to cast off the whole tangle, not to visit his father, to make innocent love to his wife and take his sons for a walk on the common, as an ordinary paterfamilias. The story analyses the guilt of those born too late for heroism, and also the obsession with the images of the immediate past.

Julian Barnes's *Staring at the Sun* has the same deliberately restricted world. It tells the tale of Jean Serjeant, a very ordinary girl, who is born before the war, gets married, has a son, and is an old woman in 2020. The novel, in which little happens, is a meditation on life, death, and the impossibility of immortality. Its central image is that of the opening pages, in which a Spitfire pilot called Prosser, in 1941, comes back from the French coast and dives so steeply that he sees the sun rise twice

> the same sun coming up from the same place across the same sea. Once more, Prosser put aside caution and just watched: the orange globe, the yellow bar, the horizon's shelf, the serene air, and the smooth weightless lift of the sun as it rose from the waves for the second time that morning. It was an ordinary miracle he would never forget.[12]

The idea that Barnes relates to this 'ordinary miracle' is that of La Rochefoucauld, 'Le soleil ni la mort ne se peuvent regarder fixement.'[13] The sun rising is simply life; the Spitfire is in a sense death, or at least mortality. Prosser has lost his nerve in fire. Jean's son, Gregory makes balsa-wood aeroplanes. Jean, watching him, makes images in her head of his future, of the relations of the generations.

> They stand on our shoulders, she thought, and with the added height, they can see farther. They can also, from up there, look back at the path we have taken, and avoid making the mistakes we did. We are handing something on to them – a torch, a relay baton, a burden. As we weaken, they grow strong: the young man carries the ancestor on his back and leads his own child by the hand.
>
> But she had also seen enough to doubt all this. These images appeared strong, but they were made only of balsa-wood and

27

tissue-paper. As often as not the parent stands on the child's shoulders, crushing it into the soft soil . . . And so Jean also wished for her son the negative things, the avoidances. May you avoid poverty, misery, disease. May you be unremarkable. May you do the best you can but not chase impossibilities . . . May you not get burnt, even once.

In later years she wondered if these wan ambitions had communicated themselves to Gregory.

The tone is sober, deliberately banal. Gregory's model planes are built to look at, not to fly. He is afraid of them crashing. He paints them in bright colours – 'a scarlet Hurricane, a purple Spitfire, an orange Messerschmitt and an emerald Zero' – 'with its joke colouring and silly yellow wheels it had ended up as no more than a child's toy'. But finally he makes a gold Vampire, which flies and crashes. Jean finds its engine in a hedge, and Gregory makes a metaphor of it as the soul, which 'might be superior to the body without being different from it as some people imagined. The soul might be made of a more durable material – aluminium as against balsa wood, say – but one which would eventually prove just as susceptible to time and space and gravity . . .'

Gregory goes into Life Insurance, and in the futuristic end of the novel, just before the aged Jean goes up to look twice at the sun herself, interrogates a computer about God and Immortality. We are now in a world of humane euthanasia and the possibility of needing to choose death. Gregory receives from the computer, amongst a lot of odd fragments of pseudo-wisdom, the remark of Kierkegaard's that is the epigraph to Part III of the novel – 'Immortality is no learned question.' This takes us back to the epigraph to the first part, a quotation from a letter of Olga Knipper to Chekhov – 'You ask me what life is? It is like asking what a carrot is. A carrot is a carrot, and nothing more is known.'

Something that surprised me in the war novels of the post-war generation was the fact that the interest common to all of them, in linear time and the finiteness of the single biological life, is always accompanied by some teasing or puzzling image of infinity and indestructibility. The novels look back before the authors' births, and seem to need to project their narrative into a future far beyond the time of writing. Jean, in *Staring at the Sun*, sees her life as a series of Incidents, and the narrative is fragmented and disconnected, linking them tenuously. Her final aeroplane flight to see the sun set twice as Prosser saw it rise twice, is, she thinks the last 'Incident' she will have. It consists, like the first, of a recurrence, a repetition, a doubled experience of the beginning and ending that the sun makes of the days of the earth, which is 'an ordinary miracle', not an experience of timelessness, but an experience, in its repetition, that juggles the mind into cyclical time, and out of the linear time of biology and entropy. In the same way, in *Shuttlecock*, Swift sets the bad, and linear, repeating pattern of the narrator's handing on of the pain of the war, against an image of indestructibility, a series of the adventures of the 'Bionic Man', a self-renewing hero his children watch on the television. At the height of his madness the narrator returns television and bionic man to the shop, to deny the children the narrative of renewal, one might almost say – or the illusion of immortality. The false eternity inhabited by his vegetative father is perhaps the bad side of the false eternity of the Bionic Man. At the end, after the reconciliation and the casting-off, the Bionic Man (and heroism) are allowed to return.

Related to *Shuttlecock* and to *Staring at the Sun* is a brief novel by Pat Barker, *The Man Who Wasn't There*. This is the story of twelve-year-old Colin whose mother is a waitress who dresses up as a fawn, and who does not know who his father is or was. Colin lives increasingly in a fantasy-world, constructed from films, of secret agents and torture and betrayal behind enemy lines in France. Like Gregory he spends his time constructing miniature bombers and fighters out of fragile balsa-wood. He creeps into cinemas, without paying, and recognises his mother's emotional account of his father's departure as part of the crew of a bomber that never came back, as simply the plot of the last film he saw. He is followed by a sinister man in black, who may be his father, or a child molester, or a phantasm. When he finally comes face to face with this figure late in the book – having had a fright when he discovered he was psychic at a séance – it is another version of the projected future, and he realises that the man is his future self, who has been unable to let go of the past, or the pain of the uncertainty of his father's identity. (He slowly comes to see that his mother *simply doesn't know* who his father was.) This novel, like the others, is about the necessity to let go of the past, including the heady fantasies of its violence and urgency. Colin's war-daydreams are both a resource and a danger to him, like the father's book in *Shuttlecock*. They are also a formal exploration of the structure of his consciousness and anxieties – funny and sharp.

In this context I should like to look briefly at Barker's much more substantial war novels, the *Regeneration* trilogy, which go much further back in time, and recreate the world and the language of the First World War. I believe Barker's trilogy is much the best, and formally much the most interesting, of the flourishing and increasing number of novels about the First World War in Britain. In 1981 D.M. Thomas published *The White Hotel*, a phantasmagoric novel in many voices which recreated a Freudian analysis of a lost trauma, and also retold the horrors of Babi Yar, in words so derivative that – despite our sophistication, even then, about faction, postmodern quotation, 'framing' truth with fiction, or interweaving the two in the way I admire immensely in Peter Everett – it was accused of plagiarism, and felt to gain its chief shock from someone else's purloined text. But Thomas's bravura, and only partly successful use of the Freudian vision of the concealed and suppressed narratives of past shocks, made me see just how startling and formally inventive was Barker's decision to use the real army psychologist, W.H.R. Rivers as her central character – along with Siegfried Sassoon, the real poet, and Billy Prior, an invented officer risen from the northern working-class. Freud wrote *Beyond the Pleasure Principle* because he could not understand why shell-shocked soldiers dreamed repeatedly the horrors they had lived through – dreams for Freud, until then, had been wish-fulfilment. Dreams, re-presentations, either paralysed the patient, or made it possible for him to live through the repetitions and into a future self. Rivers cures the shell-shocked by taking them through their traumas until they can live with them – and then he sends them back to the Front, and the death many of them desire, with their men, as the only possible conclusion of the horror. Barker uses Prior to explore the enormous shifts and rifts in the structure of society, sexuality, and the psyche brought about by the war. She shows women empowered and rejuvenated by work, however dreadful. She shows men becoming bisexual, or revealing homosexuality they might have suppressed or hidden. She shows the inadequacy of art with a quick description of a performance of Oscar Wilde's *Salome*, where the soldiers see the severed head of the Baptist not tragic or terrible, but simply grotesque and ludicrous – though Wilde's epicene Salome is much to the point in the lives of their world. I have not time to show the local precision of Barker's understanding of both people and larger issues – her story is told simply, and realistically, and the difficult sanity and responsibility of her adult men is a greater achievement than Thomas's erotic spillage of risky description. A German professor said to me that he had been told that the novels were 'simply about the ideology of the feminisation of society brought about by the war'. Barker can recognise ideology when she meets it, but it is not what she is doing – she has a true novelist's curiosity about whole people, thinking, feeling, and acting, with complex constraints of background, personal history and language. Indeed, I think that she found her great subject partly because she was a woman avoiding the constraints of prescribed feminist subject-matter. She is interested in men, she cares for and about men, and her book is about maleness, combativeness, the values of courage and the dangers of cruelty and violence. Rivers puts together the selves, the frail identities, of his soldiers, with love and respect, and then they die. The novel is haunted, not as the Second World War ones, including Barker's, are, by projections of the far future, but by the presence of returning ghosts, most of whom were sons who would not be fathers.

Freud's work, and Rivers's, is about the constitution of the Self, which was the great theme of the modernist novel. I believe that post-modern writers are returning to historical fiction because the idea of writing about the Self is felt to be worked out, or precarious, or because these writers are attracted by the idea that perhaps we have no such thing as an organic, discoverable, single Self. We are perhaps no more than a series of disjunct sense-impressions, remembered Incidents, shifting bits of knowledge, opinion, ideology and stock responses. We like historical persons because they are unknowable, only partly available to the imagination, and we find this occluded quality attractive. After the disappearance of the Immortal Soul, the disappearance of the developed and coherent Self. Proust, Joyce and Mann were disintegrating their immense consciousnesses as fast as they integrated them. We think we are like Olga Knipper's carrot. The joking, self-deprecating plainness of *Shuttlecock* and *Staring at the Sun* is to do with a sense of the diminished importance of the Self, which is no longer the battleground of cosmic forces of good and evil, honour and betrayal, but a school for minor virtues – a little courage, a lost delicacy of human kindness.

I'd like to end on two novels about false eternities, about Selves and Souls, both war novels of a strange and original kind, William Golding's *Pincher Martin* and Martin Amis's *Time's Arrow*. Both in a sense are novels which work on a single conceit, and both conceits work to provide an image of the annihilation of linear time. Both play tricks on the reader. Golding's is a modernist metaphor with its roots in literature much older than the realist novel, in spiritual allegories like *Pilgrim's Progress* or the Book of Job. Amis's is a postmodernist construction, a deliberately artificial and witty device. Both are about the unmaking of the soul, or self, or conscious mind, or living being.

Pincher Martin recounts the struggle for survival of its unpleasant eponymous hero, who is stranded on a rock in the Atlantic after his warship has been torpedoed. It describes his efforts to survive – eating nasty jellies, attempting to make his bowels work, to make a signal with stones – and his memories, which are of his own small greeds and large treacheries. It recounts the disintegration of his sense of himself. Martin was an actor, a series of characters, with a knot of greed at the centre.

> How can I have a complete identity without a mirror? This is what has changed me. Once I was a man with twenty photographs of myself – myself as this and that with the signature scrawled across the bottom right-hand corner as a stamp and seal. Even when I was in the Navy there was the photograph in my identity card so that every now and then I could look and see who I was. Or perhaps I did not even need to look, but was content to wear the card next to my heart, secure in the knowledge that it was there, proof of me in the round. There were mirrors too, triple mirrors, more separate than the three lights in this window . . . I could spy myself and assess the impact of Christopher Martin Hadley on the world. I could find the assurance of my solidity in the bodies of other

people by warmth and caresses and triumphant flesh. I could be a character in a body. But now I am this thing in here, a great many aches of bruised flesh and these lobsters on the rock. The three lights of my window are not enough to identify me however sufficient they were in the world. But there were other people to describe me to myself – they fell in love with me, they applauded me, they caressed this body, they defined it for me. There were the people I got the better of, people who disliked me, people who quarrelled with me. Here I have nothing to quarrel with. I am in danger of losing definition. I am an album of snapshots, random, a whole show of trailers of old films. The most I know of my face is the scratch of bristles, an itch, a sense of tingling warmth.[14]

The fragmentation of Pincher Martin is not the fragmentation of the postmodern individual – it is a mixture of dissolution and the insecurity of the actor, the incomplete person, in a world where soul and self are still values. His clinging to a sense of his 'centre' as he refuses to die turns out to have been a metaphor which produced the whole island from a decaying tooth in a prolonged 'eternal instant'. He had not even time to kick off his seaboots, say the corpse-collectors. The Self has to be dissolved by apocalyptic lightning, which reveals the rocks as painted water and 'papery stuff'.

There was nothing but the centre and the claws. They were huge and strong and inflamed to red. They closed on each other. They contracted. They were outlined like a night sign against the absolute nothingness and they gripped their whole strength into each other . . .

The lightning crept in. The centre was unaware of anything but the claws and the threat. It focussed its awareness on the crumbled serrations and the blazing red. The lightning came forward. Some of the lines pointed towards the centre, waiting for the moment when they could pierce it. Others lay against the claws, playing over them, prying for a weakness, wearing them away in a compassion that was timeless and without mercy.

Here again is an image of timelessness, of eternal recurrence, set against biological finitude. I want to compare this with Martin Amis's novel, *Time's Arrow* (1991), which takes its title from the opposition of the idea of linear time (which we derive from biological time) moving always from beginning to end, and in one direction, and Time's Cycle, the idea of recurrence, of repetitions like the cycle of the seasons, for instance, or the regular rising of the sun. Amis has invented the metaphysical conceit of reversing Time's Arrow, so that it points backwards, and his novel tells the reversed tale of a Nazi war criminal, beginning with his secret second life as a doctor in the United States. The tale includes dialogues which provoke extraordinary double takes, as they mean one thing read forwards and another backwards. The narrator is not the criminal, Tod Friendly, who rebecomes Odilo Unverdorben, but is perhaps in some sense his soul, who shares his body. In the hospital (where in reversed time the doctor restores the cured to their original pain) the narrator denies that his co-habitant is 'doing good work'.

> If I died, would he stop? If I am his soul, and there were soul-loss or soul-death, would that stop him? Or would it make him even freer?
>
> . . . You can't end yourself. Not here. I am familiar with the idea of suicide. But once life is running, you can't end it. You aren't at liberty to do that. We're all here for the duration. Life *will* end. I know exactly how long I've got. It looks like forever. I feel unique and eternal. Immortality consumes me – and me only.[15]

In the Camp, since everything is backwards, Odilo and his secret sharer are bringing Jews to life, reconstituting families, sending them back into society.

> I would never claim that Auschwitz-Birkenau-Monowitz was good to look at. Or to listen to, or to smell, or to taste or to touch. There was, among my colleagues there, a genuine though desultory quest for greater elegance. I can understand that word, and all its yearning: *elegant*. Not for its elegance did I come to love the evening sky, hellish red with the gathering

souls. Creation is easy. Also ugly. *Hier ist kein warum.* Here there is no why. Here there is no when, no how, no where. Our preternatural purpose? To dream a race. To make a people from the weather. From thunder and from lightning. With gas, with electricity, with shit, with fire.

This is both savage satire and something more, a visionary moment. The novel does not stop with the creation of the Jews from fire. It works its way back through the life of Odilo Unverdorben, to the points of birth and conception – where Odilo's father is 'about to come in and kill him with his body', and in that sense is like a psychoanalysis, like those shadowed in Pat Barker and D.M. Thomas, or in Sammy Mountjoy's self-examination in *Free Fall*, looking for the source of evil in time, backwards through memory. Amis's burning light of the unmaking, or creation, of the Jews, is related to Pincher Martin's probing lines of light made of 'a compassion that was timeless and without mercy'. It is and it is not far from Elizabeth Bowen's blitzed London, Henry Green's beautiful inferno, and the sun rising twice and setting twice in an ordinary miracle in *Staring at the Sun*.

Forefathers

This essay is about the extraordinary variety of distant pasts British writers are inventing, and the extraordinary variety of forms in which those pasts have been constructed. I want to begin with the beginnings of some nineteenth-century historical novels. Here is *A Tale of Two Cities*.

> It was the best of times, it was the worst of times, it was the age of wisdom, it was the age of foolishness, it was the epoch of belief, it was the epoch of incredulity, it was the season of Light, it was the season of Darkness, it was the spring of hope, it was the winter of despair, we had everything before us, we had nothing before us, we were all going direct to heaven, we were all going direct the other way – in short, the period was so far like the present period, that some of its noisiest authorities insisted on its being received, for good or evil, in the superlative degree of comparison only.

And here is the Proem to George Eliot's *Romola*, which is a vision of Europe from the planing viewpoint of the Angel of the dawn.

> The great river-courses which have shaped the lives of men have hardly changed; and those other streams, the life-currents that ebb and flow in human hearts, pulsate to the same great needs, the same great loves and terrors. As one thought follows another in the slow wake of the dawn, we are impressed with the broad sameness of the human lot, which

never alters in the main headings of its history – hunger and labour, seed-time and harvest, love and death.

Both these novelists, in a kind of biblical rhetoric, emphasise samenesses and continuities between the past and the present. Both were writing close to historical texts that had moved them – Carlyle's French Revolution, and Sismondi's *History of the Italian Republics*. Both believed they could know the past through its analogies with the present, and both wrote very Victorian books, instantly recognisable Victorian books, about their chosen historical crises. Walter Scott's projects were more complex, and his historical intelligence sharper. Ian Duncan's excellent new edition of *Rob Roy* connects Scott's invention of a literary Highlands with James Macpherson's forged 'Ossian' poems. Scott's narrator is writing his memoir of Rob Roy during the publication of the Ossian poems, which, Duncan says

> defined a new cultural position of *inauthenticity*, somewhere between translation and forgery, which would become the classic position of an 'invented tradition in modern letters'. Antiquarian reconstruction and poetic fantasy combined in the reverie of a vanished ancestral nation, grown glamorously remote and strange.

What James Buzard called Scott's mediating devices of 'translation and tourism' – English lords in kilts and tartans –

> represent, for the novel's reader, the formation of a distinctively modern kind of national subjectivity, in which the knowledge of our alienation from 'authentic' cultural identities accompanies our privileged repossession of those lost identities as aesthetic effects.[1]

There has been a general feeling during my writing life that we cannot know the past – often extended into the opinion that we therefore should not write about it. The sense we have that Eliot's Florence and Dickens's Paris mob are part of their Victorian English vision has contributed to this, whilst postmodernist writers like Jeanette Winterson have felt free to create their own fantasy pasts from odd details of names, events and places. If we can't know, we may invent, and anything goes. There has also been a complex discussion of the rhetoric of historical writing itself, which has included both political discussion of the priorities and cultural assumptions of the historians, and structural analysis of their narrative and language. Historians have become suspicious of history which concentrates on the fates and motives of individuals. Hayden White observes that novelists like Balzac and Flaubert could believe they were writing 'history' because the forms of their fictions coincided with the forms of nineteenth-century histories, written by bourgeois historians, who believed that their historical narratives were a form of science. The French *Annales* historians, he says, reject narrative history because it is inherently 'dramatising' or 'novelising' (and concerned with past politics). White remarks that

> One suspects that it is not the dramatic nature of novels that is at issue but a distaste for a genre of literature that puts human agents rather than impersonal processes at the centre of interest and suggests that such agents have some significant control over their own destinies.[2]

Recent historians like Simon Schama have made deliberate and self-conscious attempts to restore narration to history – Schama's account of the French Revolution[3] was shocking partly because he reverted to portraits of 'characters' and individual lives and deaths as a way of narrating the events, and even suggested that the personality of Louis XVI may have had some influence on his fate. This new interest in narration can, I think, be related to the novelists' new sense of the need for, and essential interest of, storytelling, after a long period of stream-of-consciousness, followed by the fragmented, non-linear forms of the *nouveau roman* and the experimental novel. The idea that 'all history is fiction' led to a new interest in fiction as history.

There are many current forms of historical fiction – parodic and pastiche forms, forms which fake documents or incorporate real ones, mixtures of past and present, hauntings and ventriloquism, historical versions of genre fictions – Roman and mediaeval and Restoration detective stories and thrillers, both in popular literature and serious writing. The purposes of the writer can be incantatory, analytic, romantic, or stylistic. Or playful, or extravagant, or allegorical. Even the ones apparently innocently realist – Pat Barker, whom I discussed in the last essay, or Hilary Mantel, to whom I shall come in this – do not choose realism unthinkingly, but almost as an act of shocking rebellion against current orthodoxies.

I'll start with a form that may take its name from John Fowles's novel, *A Maggot*. Fowles says, 'A maggot is the larval stage of a winged creature; as is the written text, at least in the writer's hope.' But it is also a 'whimsical fancy' (*OED*) or as Fowles says of the musical maggots of the mid-eighteenth-century in which his novel is set 'written out of obsession with a theme'.[4] He says it began with a single image, of a group of riders travelling across a deserted landscape. He has also said that the reign of George II, in which it is set, is one of the patches of English history that we have not recently imagined in any depth or intensity. We have studied the time of Shakespeare and the politics and literature of the English revolution. We are familiar with the time of romantic poetry, and very knowledgeable about the nineteenth-century of the great social novels and the clash between science and religion. The pleasure both writer and reader take from Fowles's maggot, which he insists is not 'a historical novel', is the recreation of the feeling and the voices of this estranged eighteenth-century past, as though the first isolated image of travellers had called up a whole world. The novel contains a whole 'Historical Chronicle' in month-by-month reproductions from the *Gentleman's Magazine* for 1736, full of true facts, historical nuggets about long-vanished bonesetters and gamekeepers, hangings and highwaymen. The novel is a tale of whoredom and witchcraft and provides a fictive ancestry for Mother Ann Lee, the founder of the Shakers. Fowles's own narration is a triumphant exercise in ventriloquism, transcripts of imagined court proceedings and records. The novel ends with a vision, in a cave, of a 'maggot' which is clearly a kind of space-ship from some future, or other world, luminous and containing a new kind of people. In a sense, despite the wonderful invention and recreation of past syntax and past incidents, the maggot turns on its own metaphor – which at the end Fowles describes as being one for 'that founding stage or moment in all religions, however blind, stale and hidebound they later become, which saw a superseded skeleton must be destroyed, or at least adapted to a new world'. Mother Ann Lee's 'Logos' he says, was the 'almost divine maggot' of her spiritual world. The initial vision of the unknown past figures and their slow progress across a lost landscape is deeply moving in a way I can't wholly explain. The rest of the novel is experienced as an appendage to a momentary vision. Perhaps it is moving because it epitomises our desire to call up the past, and simultaneously the difficulty, and the fragmentary nature, of any attempt to do so.

Jeanette Winterson's *The Passion*, set in the Napoleonic Wars, is also a maggot, a fantasia derived from the fictive pasts of Calvino, and turning, like *A Maggot*, on the punning metaphor in its title. It begins with Napoleon's passion for chicken, and goes on to a fairy-tale chronicle of erotic and violent events, accompanied by pithy sayings, like an allegory. Here are the recruits to the Napoleonic army.

> Most of these recruits aren't seventeen and they're asked to do in a few weeks what vexes the best philosophers for a lifetime; that is, to gather up their passion for life and make sense of it in the face of death.
>
> They don't know how but they do know how to forget, and little by little they put aside the burning summer in their bodies and all they have instead is lust and rage.[5]

The word 'passion' also stands at the centre of Christianity. Winterson sees both passion as love and passion as suffering as functions of human sexuality. Her cross-dressing heroine sees her connection to God as

> indulging without fear the exquisite masochism of the victim. Lie beneath his lances and close your eyes. Where else could you be so in control? Not in love, certainly . . .
>
> In spite of what the monks say, you can meet God without getting up early. You can meet God lounging in the pew. The hardship is a man-made device because man cannot exist without passion. Religion is somewhere between fear and sex. And God? Truly? In his own right, without our voices speaking for him? Obsessed, I think, but not passionate.
>
> In our dreams we sometimes struggle from the oceans of

desire up Jacob's ladder to that orderly place. Then human voices wake us and we drown.

Richard Sennett, in *The Fall of Public Man*, has some very interesting things to say about the contemporary tendency for people to identify their selves with their sexuality. He writes that

> the enshrining of the body as an absolute sexual state is narcissistic because it makes sexuality exclusively an attribute of the person, a state of being rather than an activity, and therefore essentially isolated from the sexual experience the person may or may not have . . . This is one reason why, as a society shifts from eroticism to sexuality, from belief in emotional actions to belief in emotional states of being, destructive psychological forces are brought to the fore.[6]

I don't have the space to argue my case in detail, but I do think one way of describing Jeanette Winterson's imaginary pasts is that they are made to be fables of this modern self-perception. Sexuality is co-extensive and interchangeable with identity. This is different from Freudian metaphors drawn from the dreaming mind. It is not that flowers and buildings and rivers are unconscious metaphors for the body. It is conscious daydreaming, and it is knowing about its own sexual preoccupations. The pasts Winterson makes are projections of daydreams.

My final example of the 'maggot' is *Flying to Nowhere*, John Fuller's elegant fable set on an imaginary island, in an imaginary monastic community. It is both a thriller about the investigation of the vanishing corpses of pilgrims, and a metaphysical tale – sensuous and riddling – about the relations between spirit and flesh, life and matter. It opens with a horse, having leapt from a boat, dying in pain on the coast of the island. The horse's name is Saviour, but it is not saved. Later, its grieving groom thrusts his hand into its maggot-ridden flesh and feels the extraordinary heat of life. The abbot is dissecting the corpses, looking for the seat of the soul; the island's saint has a dedicated miraculous fountain, and the abbot hopes to bring back the dead, who are silting up its channels. Beauty is always next to terror, moonlit orchards to broken bones. The abbot is concerned for the life of his books, the words of the dead which are their afterlife, or perhaps their immortality. In the astounding final image the living waters have restored, not the dead men, but the dead matter – wood and leather and vellum – in the library.

Some thought of consulting the Egyptian authorities had brought him to the dangerous level of the library, where he had to struggle through the sprouting thicket of the beams, bending aside the sappy branches that sprouted from all panels of the door. Too late? What had happened to all that inscribed wisdom? Was it wasted on the fetid air in the vanishing shape of bellowing and the breath of beasts? Or had the vellum rumination already passed its cud of knowledge from the ultimate tract? Would he, if he could gain access to the library, merely slither upon a useless excrement of instruction and philosophy?

He stood with his hand upon the knotted bark of the library door in despair as it thudded against his palm with the weight of the huddled herds inside. The living books seemed to have sensed his presence: the bellowing increased as they jostled on the other side of the strained wood, and the ring of hooves on the flooded stone blended with the fresh trumpeting of panic and rebellion. Too late!

Words were indeed more enduring than the body. Mrs Ffederbompau's letter had fallen from his fingers as he had battled with the foliage, and had lain for a few minutes in the warm well water. Now small shoots of reeds pushed up from the paper, and hair-like roots wiggled to seek the lodgings of cracks in stone. Gall and insect ichor trickled down the fronds, and from the bubbling seal came a sweet stench of wax and a buzzing murmur. The Abbot stooped in sudden love to this miniature landscape which spread like a riverbank by his feet. Shapes were busy in the rushes, crawling up towards the swelling heads of the seed. Mrs Ffederbompau's last words were in his head, like a drowsy charm; and on the edge of his hearing, louder than the stampede of his library, rose for an endless moment the purposeful clamour of tiny wings.[7]

The 'maggot' in *Flying to Nowhere* turns on a metaphor of maggots, the life that feeds on death, mutability. Fuller's excellent collection of short stories, *The Worm and the Star*, turns on the same metaphors for life, death, and the unchanging light.

'Words were indeed more enduring than the body.' I want to turn now to a form of historical writing I call 'ventriloquism', to avoid the loaded moral implications of 'parody', or 'pastiche'. I have mentioned this in the context of Fowles's sustained recreation of an eighteenth-century voice, vocabulary and habit of mind in *A Maggot*. In the case of Peter Ackroyd it is the *raison d'être* of his work, much of which concerns the raising of the spirits of the dead – as in *The House of Dr Dee* – quite literally. His novels are ghostly mysteries, in which the dangerous dead shape the course of the life of the living. In Ackroyd's case – and to an extent in my own – the genre of the ghost story is used as an embodiment of the relations between readers and writers, between the living words of dead men and the modern conjurers of their spirits. Ackroyd does this in many different ingenious ways. *Chatterton*[8] is a novel about fakes and parodies – Chatterton invented a mediaeval poet and wrote his poems, the poet Meredith posed for the famous painting of the Death of Chatterton, Ackroyd's modern characters are haunted by these dead poets in reality and are themselves engaged in faking further documents which may nevertheless be 'true' works of art. *The Last Testament of Oscar Wilde* is both a loving reading and resurrection of Wilde, and a wonderful intertextual faking of his voice. *Hawksmoor* is a brilliant rendering of the voices of Nicholas Dyer in 1711, constructing London churches on an occult programme, and the modern detective, Hawksmoor, who is investigating the disappearance and murder of children. The novel turns on riddling images of circular, or eternally repeating time, closed in on itself like mirrors – in the end the two men face each other as man and image, and blend. The eighteenth-century dispute about the relative powers of the Ancients and the Moderns becomes a riddling image for the continuing life of dead writers in Dyer's mind – his spiritual designs are intended to confute the modern rationalism of Sir Christopher Wren. In a typical moment he describes a visit to Stonehenge with Wren

It was Evening now, and as the sloping Rays of the Sunne shone on the ground beyond the Stones, we could easily distinguish the sepulchral Tumuli which lie in great Numbers around there; and this Phrase occurred to me as I looked upon them: the Banks where wild Time blows. At the sight of the Shaddowes which Stonehenge now cast upon the short Grass, Sir Chris. cleared up his Countenance: Well you see Nick, *says he*, how these are Shaddowes on a known Elevation to show the equal Hours of the Day. It is easy to frame the Pillars that every Day at such a Time the Shaddowes will seem to return, *he continued*, and I am glad to say that Logarithms is a wholly British art. I shall subjoyn as a Corollary to the foregoing Remarks that Sir Chris. his Son died of a Convulsive Fitt in a foreign Land, the which News we did not receive until several months after the Events here related.

And now these Scenes return to me again, and, tho' here in my Office, I am gone backward through Time and can see the Countenance of Sir Chris. as once it was in the shaddowe of Stone-henge. Truly Time is a vast Denful of Horrour, round about which a Serpent winds and in the winding bites itself by the Tail. Now, now is the Hour, every Hour, every part of an Hour, every Moment, which in its end does begin again and never ceases to end: a beginning continuing, always ending.[9]

It is interesting to compare *Hawksmoor* with William Golding's *The Spire*, which is also about the building of churches, and also contains an image of the blood sacrifice from some earlier and darker religion buried under the stones of the new church. Golding's Sea Trilogy, written much later than *The Spire*, created a nineteenth-century diary voice, using ventriloquism and parody. The narrative voice of *The Spire*, however, is a modern voice, and the central concern is a modernist metaphor, derived from a Freudian understanding of the riddling and secret nature of human motivation. Jocelin's religious ecstasy and force of aspiration in building his spire is seen as having sexual roots – he dreams the spire springing from his loins and the cathedral as the spread body of a man. Ackroyd's interest in spirits and the occult may be as real as Golding's passionate preoccupation with the true nature of religion and evil, but his ventriloquism serves to emphasise at once the presence of the past and its distance, its difference, its death and difficult resurrection. It is interesting also to compare Ackroyd's thresholds between past and present with a recent novel by the young Scottish writer, A.L. Kennedy, *So I Am Glad*, in which a Glasgow broadcaster discovers that the new lodger in the house she lodges in is Cyrano de Bergerac, mysteriously brought back. At one level this is a genre tale, in which the dead man has to be restored to the past from which he has been propelled. But it is also about reader and writer, and storytelling. Kennedy's heroine is an unhappy sado-masochist, whose family life and professional life are loveless. Cyrano teaches her romantic love, and also goes out and fights the Glasgow gangs as he once fought duel upon duel in seventeenth-century France. Like Chatterton Cyrano is a composite creation – a seventeenth-century wit and thinker who was turned into a Romantic hero by Rostand – Kennedy has done her homework, and knows the work of the real Cyrano as well as Rostand's romance. Her novel asks, what is the difference between love and courage in twentieth-century Glasgow and seventeenth-century France? It gives no easy answers, but is certainly a tale of a love affair between the living and the dead.

Which brings me briefly to my own novel, *Possession*, which is about all these things, ventriloquism, love for the dead, the presence of literary texts as the voices of persistent ghosts or spirits. I have always been haunted by Browning's images of his own historical poems as acts of *resurrection* – he compared himself, in *The Ring and the Book*, both to Faust and to Elisha, who breathed life into a dead corpse. What I should like to say here about my own text is that ventriloquism became necessary because of what I felt was the increasing gulf between current literary criticism and the words of the literary texts it in some sense discusses. Modern criticism is powerful and imposes its own narratives and priorities on the writings it uses as raw material, source, or jumping-off point. It may be interested in feminist, or Lacanian, or marxist, or post-colonial narratives and vocabularies. Or it may play forcefully with the words of the writer, interjecting its own punning meanings. You can discover African obeah women and racist fear in Keats's *Lamia* by noting one description of the possible African origin of lamias in Lemprière's Dictionary which Keats used, or you may find anal obsession in Coriolanus by observing the ending of his name and ignoring the fact that multitudes of Latin adjectives end in 'anus'. St Paul's fierce claim to liberty – 'civis romanus sum' – was presumably also a revelation of anal obsessiveness. Such secondary cleverness distresses both the reader and the writer in me. As an innocent reader I learned to listen, again and again, to texts until they had revealed their whole shape, their articulation, the rhythms of their ideas and feelings. This was reinforced by having to be examined on texts I had learned, at length, by heart – nowadays students have open books. As a writer I know very well that a text is all the words that are in it, and not only those words, but the other words that precede it, haunt it, and are echoed in it – as Ackroyd echoed Oberon, punning on wild time, or earlier Winterson casually quoted T.S. Eliot on human voices which wake us, and we drown. Her 1980s Napoleonic Venetian can hear the voice of a 1920s American poet. A nice example of this kind of deliberate intertextual anachronism appears in Julian Rathbone's novel about Harold, *The Last English King*. Rathbone says in his preface that 'occasionally characters, and even the narrator, let slip quotations or near quotations of later writers or make oblique references to later times . . . Some will find this irritating. For reasons I find difficult to explain it amuses me, and may amuse others. But it also serves a more serious purpose – to place the few years spanned by the book in a continuum which leads forwards as well as back . . .' So his readers will find two travellers discussing the splendours of eleventh-century Byzantium. 'What is it all for?' one asks.

His new friend shrugged.
'Monuments of their own magnificence?' he suggested with dismissive wryness.[10]

This amuses and moves me too, for obscure reasons to do with unexpected connection, with the flexibility of linguistic forms.

I was recently asked to contribute to a collection of essays which explored ways of standing out against the idea that we cannot read the Victorians, but always and only our own idea of them. I said that writing Victorian words in Victorian contexts, in a Victorian order, and in Victorian relations of one word to the next was the only way I could think of to show one could hear the Victorian dead. *Possession* is not innocent evocation of voices, for the pure pleasure of recreating the Victorian rhythms by which I am haunted. It has its cunning – Christabel LaMotte's *Melusina* was written because I had heard a talk by the French feminist, Luce Iragaray, on powerful women who were neither virgins nor mothers. It was written to conform with a feminist interpretation of the imaginary poem – an interpretation I had in fact written before writing the text itself. It was the gulf between the vocabularies and the 'feel' of the words that pleased me, and made writing the poem necessary. And before writing the poem, I read the dead writers Christabel read, the French monk, Jean d'Arras, John Keats and John Milton, whose snakes and Lamias inform her writing. For the Victorians were not simply Victorian. They read their past, and resuscitated it.

I'd like to end what I have to say about ventriloquism by mentioning a text I love for its sheer bravura love of words and language – though like everything I've discussed it's also about life, death, time and timelessness, very directly. It is Anthony Burgess's *Abba Abba* in which he recounts the death of Keats in Rome, and imagines a fictional encounter between the scurrilous and devout Roman sonneteer, Giuseppe Gioachino Belli and the dying Englishman. Keats, and Burgess himself, translate Belli's sonnets into English. Burgess, describing Keats's too early death, brings him to life and makes his readers relive his death. The words, ABBA ABBA, are the words Christ spoke on the Cross, calling on the father who was silent. They are also the mirroring, closed form of the octave of a sonnet, of which Burgess's Belli sees a Platonic form, an absolute that he calls God.

> 'The sonnet form must have existed *in potentia* from the beginning, but it was made flesh with such as Petrarch . . . One may vary the rhymes a little but the essential shape will remain. The wordless sonnet that still rhymes, that says nothing, having no words, but yet speaks. It says: I am this but I am also this. In my eight lines X, in my six lines Y, but in my total fourteen ever the unity, the ultimate statement whose meaning is itself. What is this, your eminence, but the true image of God?'

'Heretical, yes, you were right when you said that. You talk of an abstraction, a ghost.'

'I talk of an ultimate reality. And through the glimmering of it I have given you, a soul may speak to a soul.'

ABBA ABBA also repeats Anthony Burgess's initials, and is written on his tombstone, where Keats had 'Here lies one whose name was writ in water.' It is the form of the octave of a sonnet, a repetition of a cry, half the abstract idea of Burgess's notion of an incarnate timeless perfection.

Possession plays serious games with the variety of possible forms of narrating the past – the detective story, the biography, the mediaeval verse Romance, the modern romantic novel, and Hawthorne's fantastic historical Romance in between, the campus novel, the Victorian third-person narration, the epistolary novel, the forged manuscript novel, and the primitive fairy tale of the three women, filtered through Freud's account of the theme in his paper on the Three Caskets. I'd like to look now at two other novels which play serious games with the idea of narrative itself – Julian Barnes's *A History of the World in 10½ Chapters* and Graham Swift's *Waterland*. *A History of the World* imitates various forms as it tells and retells stories of human danger and survival, cataclysm and escape. Its overarching form is the narrative that has shaped Western civilisation for centuries – the biblical narrative in which both cataclysm and escape are the product of the relation between human acts, human good and evil and Divine vengeance, or alternatively, protection. It opens with a comic-fantastic account of the journey of Noah's Ark, by a narrator who turns out to be a stowaway woodworm, and ends in a comfortable post-death semi-eternal duration. From Covenant to the promised eternal life. Within that frame various short tales depict floating perils – a tour-ship hijacked by terrorists, an ecologist fleeing an irradiated world in a coracle, survivors of the wreck of the *Titanic* and of being swallowed by a sperm-whale, Géricault's painting of 'The Raft of the *Medusa*', and a painstaking account of the precise events that led to the incident from which that Romantic image of hope and despair was formed. There are recurrent searches for the lost Ark – by, for instance a nineteenth-century woman explorer with a religious temperament, whose body is found in a later episode by Spike Tiggler, American astronaut and evangelist. The tapping of the death-watch beetle echoes elegantly from episode to episode, and there is one bizarre and brilliant excerpt from an ecclesiastical trial in Besançon in 1520, where the beetles, or *bestioles*, are on trial for the destruction of the Bishop's throne, which led to the fall and subsequent imbecility of the Bishop. They are threatened with expulsion from the village, condemnation, anathema, and excommunication. In Chapter 6, 'The Mountain', both religious Amanda and her dying father hear the beetles (whose tapping is a mating call).

> Where Amanda discovered in the world divine intent, benevolent order and rigorous justice, her father had seen only chaos, hazard and malice. Yet they were both examining the same world . . . Amanda once asked him to consider the domestic condition of the Fergusson family, who lived together with strong bonds of affection, and declare whether they too were the consequence of chaos, hazard and malice. Colonel Fergusson, who could not quite bear to inform his daughter that the human family sprang from the same impulse which animates a beetle striking its head against the walls of its box, replied that in his view the Fergussons were a happy accident.[11]

This passage contrasts the Darwinian explanation of events with the orthodox religious one – I'll come back to that particular narrative form in the next essay. In this novel it sits beside other comments on the interpretation of the human story.

A *History of the World* comments from time to time on the nature of history, and the relations between history and fiction. There is a 'Parenthesis' (the half-chapter) between Chapters 8 and 9, which opens with a discussion of love, writing about love, and survival, and moves on to a discussion of the nature of history, writing about history, and love. I shall come back to love in the essay on Darwinian fictions. Here is what Barnes has to say about history and storytelling.

> History isn't what happened. History is just what historians tell us. There was a pattern, a plan, a movement, expansion,

the march of democracy; it is a tapestry, a flow of events, a complex narrative, connected, explicable. One good story leads to another. First it was kings and archbishops with some offstage divine tinkering, then it was the march of ideas and the movements of masses, then little local events which mean something bigger, but all the time it's connections, progress, meaning, this led to this, this happened because of this. And we, the readers of history, the sufferers from history, we scan the pattern for hopeful conclusions, for the way ahead. And we cling to history as a series of salon pictures, conversation pieces whose participants we can easily imagine back into life, when all the time it's more like a multi-media collage, with paint applied by decorator's roller rather than camel-hair brush.

The history of the world? Just voices echoing in the dark; images that burn for a few centuries and then fade; stories, old stories that sometimes seem to overlap; strange links, impertinent connections . . . We make up a story to cover up the facts we don't know or can't accept; we keep a few true facts and spin a new story round them. Our panic and our pain are only eased by soothing fabulation; we call it history.

There's one thing I'll say for history. It's very good at finding things. We try to cover them up but history doesn't let go. It's got time on its side, time and science. We bury our victims in secrecy (strangled princelings, irradiated reindeer) but history discovers what we did to them. We lost the *Titanic*, forever it seemed, in the squid-ink depths, but they turned it up. They found the wreck of the *Medusa* not long ago, off the coast of Mauretania. There wasn't any hope of salvage, they knew that; and all they salvaged after a hundred and seventy-five years were a few copper nails from the frigate's hull and a couple of cannon. But they went and found it just the same.

Barnes's image of 'salon pictures' as imagined history connects to his startling account of the painting of 'The Raft of the *Medusa*'. He asks 'How do you turn catastrophe into art?' and answers himself at first ironically, in the tone of voice in which he has reduced history to fragments and oddly isolated or bizarrely connected incidents.

How do you turn catastrophe into art?

Nowadays the process is automatic. A nuclear plant explodes? We'll have a play on the London stage within a year. A President is assassinated? You can have the book or the film or the filmed book or the booked film. War? Send in the novelists. A series of gruesome murders? Listen for the tramp of the poets. We have to understand it, of course, this catastrophe; to understand it, we have to imagine it, so we need the imaginative arts. But we also need to justify and forgive it, this catastrophe, however minimally.

His account of the painting moves from science and fact to an imaginative description of the ferocious energy of Géricault's painted wind and waves and human terror, and out into the need to imagine catastrophe and the effects of time and woodworm on the physical nature of Géricault's pigments and frame. It is an ironised vision of Romantic history and Romantic art, but the true terror is there in both painting and description.

In the essay on war novels I remarked on the oddly recurring need for these images of past history to contain images of eternity, the far future, or cyclical time. *A History of the World* ends in a ruefully funny afterlife, outside time and history, where a kind of everyman has all his desires fulfilled – food, golf scores, meeting Hitler and Shakespeare, sex and so on. When he decides he needs to be judged, which is what he expected, he is taken before an official who tells him, 'You're OK'. After a time, timelessness or infinite duration begins to pall. He learns that most inhabitants, sooner or later, let go, give up, go away. It is like a mildly, ruefully comic version of the drama at the end of *Pincher Martin*. Or of the trapped dead and live men in eternal confrontation or melding in *Hawksmoor*. It is another example of the need for images of historical time to contain their opposites.

Graham Swift's *Waterland*, like *A History of the World*, has many modes of narration. It is told by a schoolteacher, whose class refuses to be interested in the French Revolution, and whose headmaster is trying to abolish the teaching of history in his school for progressive reasons. The stories told are the simplest forms of narration – personal tales of the narrator's family history, local tales of the history of the fens where he grew up, ghost stories, economic history of the growth of the beer industry, military stories of the effects (and non-effects) of world wars on these marshy backwaters. There is a murder mystery and a tragedy, there are ancestors and incest, and long causal chains that stretch back in time. There is also the natural history of the eels, whose origins are unknown. The narrative voice is *faux-naif*. It begins with the traditional 'Once upon a time' and sets out to tell the tale of a history teacher in the future, whose life 'went wrong' and whose current profession is recapitulating the ineradicable past.[12]

The narrator, and to a certain extent the novelist, have a quibbling pedagogic tone; the fairy-story formulas are used in a heavy-handed way, but then the character is pedagogic and heavy-handed. *Waterland* gets much of its emotional force from being a novel about the slow movement of the past in a slow, undramatic landscape, and contrasting that with the general apprehension at the time when it was written, that the world was about to end in a nuclear winter. This apprehension is embodied in a rebellious boy called Price. Price, like the rebels of Burgess's *Clockwork Orange* uses corpse-white make-up. He interrupts the narrator's lesson on the French Revolution, and asserts that History is only a 'fairytale' and that all the matters is the present. The narrator observes that Price is here echoing the sentiments of 1789. Price then goes on to state that the only important thing about History is that it has probably reached its end. The narrator leaves the discussion of the French Revolution, and its hypothetical New Beginning, to tell his own story to his class, beginning again 'Once upon a time . . .'

At the beginning of this essay I quoted Dickens's novel about the French Revolution, which was inspired by Carlyle's history. I'd now like to look at three completely different novels set in the time of the Revolution simply to celebrate the variety of the historical imagination of living writers. If it is true that our ideas of the past are formed by our ideas of the present, we might expect to find our paradigms of the Revolution to be related to the ideas of Revolution of the turbulent sixties of the student revolutionaries, or to the historiography of the Left. Hayden White remarks that Fredric

Jameson is interested in fictional narratives because his political beliefs derive from a Marxism which is a master narrative whose amplitude allows us to 'unite all the individual stories of societies, groups, and cultures into a single great collective *story* . . . the collective struggle to wrest a realm of Freedom from a realm of Necessity . . . vital episodes in a single vast unfinished *plot*: 'The history of all hitherto existing society is the history of class struggle . . .' [Jameson][13] François Furet, writing about the French Left's idea of 1789 as the mythic origin of modern society, the forerunner of the Russian Revolution, gives his definition of ideology, in a world which according to him, 'was ever ready to place ideas above actual history, as if it were called upon to restructure a fragmented society by means of its own concepts'.[14]

> Here I am using the term ideology to designate the two sets of beliefs that, to my mind, constitute the very bedrock of revolutionary consciousness. The first is that all personal problems and all moral or intellectual matters have become political; that there is no human misfortune not amenable to a political solution. The second is that, since everything can be known and changed, there is a perfect fit between action, knowledge and morality. That is why the revolutionary militants identified their private lives with their public ones and with the defence of their ideas.[15]

Furet argues that histories which claim revolutions as founding events in the societies of which they are part inevitably commemorate the revolution in terms of its perceived presence in the society – a royalist commemoration would deplore lost legitimacy, a 'bourgeois' commemoration would celebrate 'the founding of a national contract', and a revolutionary commemoration would celebrate the 'dynamism of the founding event and its promises for the future'.

> The result is rather odd, a kind of residual history that at each stage derives its distinct character from the part that the present plays in the different interpretations of the past. Such an exercise is undeniably useful, even salutary, for it makes us aware of the ambiguity in which historical questions are rooted

and of the ways in which they become entangled in current issues. But lest it lead to complete historical relativism, to a concept of history as subservient to the demands of society, an illusory anchor amidst uncontrollable drift, it must do more than simply state the role of the present in the history of the Revolution; it must also be accompanied by an expertise, as precise as possible, of the constraints imposed by *our own* present.[16]

Simon Schama's *Citizens* caused a great deal of excitement by making a deliberate return to the use of storytelling and characters in the writing of history. He learned from Richard Cobb, he says in his preface, 'to see the Revolution not as a march of abstractions and ideologies but as a human event of complicated and often tragic outcomes'. The narrative of *Citizens* 'weaves between the private and the public lives of the citizens who appear on its pages. This is done not only in an attempt to understand their motivation more deeply than pure public utterance allows, but also because many of them, often to their ruin, saw their own lives as a seamless whole, their calendar of birth, love, ambition and death imprinted on the almanac of great events.' In this sense too, he says, his tale 'opts for chaotic authenticity over the commanding neatness of historical convention'.[17] The imaginative power of Schama's history is so great that for a long time I didn't read Hilary Mantel's novel, *A Place of Greater Safety* (which came out in 1992, three years after *Citizens*) though Mantel had been writing it for a long time. It is an apparently straightforward, realist narrative, covering the lives and thoughts of Camille Desmoulins, Danton, Robespierre, and their wives and lovers, in close detail, recreating the intellectual and emotional turmoil of the time both on the grand scale and with precise images of small, local details of pain, excitement, curiosity, terror and desire. It has just as powerful an emotional and aesthetic effect on its reader as *Citizens*, and a completely different one. It tells what Schama cannot tell, because he cannot know it, although both writers use the same evidence. The writer of fiction is at liberty to invent – as the historian and the biographer are not. Schama's fiction, mixed with documentary, in *Dead Certainties* lacks the dramatic power and imaginative grasp of his history, as the postmodern dialogues between biographer and subject Ackroyd inserted into his Dickens biography seemed trivial and false beside the mystery of the known facts and the unknown nature of the life being told. I said earlier that there is a new aesthetic energy to be gained from the borderlines of fact and the unknown. Hilary Mantel, like Pat Barker, writes old-fashioned psychological narrative which is the imaginative form she gives to the lives of real, partially known men. In both cases, the imaginative closeness of the narration feels less like a discarded style than a new and shocking experiment. This kind of novel – especially after Schama – on this kind of subject ought to be illegitimate. In fact it works wonderfully. Although Mantel's novel, like Barker's trilogy, is 'conventional' on the surface, any writer looking closely at the narrative choices made on each page, the juxtapositions of events, the gaps, the angle of narration, will find many new and admirable things. Mantel quotes Robespierre early in the novel – he said in 1793 'History is fiction'[18] and later embodies the remark in her imagined text. Her fiction is fiction – it is not history – although it has a historical narrator who occasionally stops the story, and sets the scene in the present tense. Her intermittent use of the historic present has something in common with Dickens's use of that tense for his impersonal narrator, describing the outside world in *Bleak House*.

> The year is now 1774. Poseurs or not, it is time to grow up. It is time to enter the public realm, the world of public acts and public attitudes. Everything that happens now will happen in the light of history. It is not a mid-day luminary but a corpse-candle to the intellect; at best, it is a second-hand lunar light, error-breeding, sand-blind and parched.
>
> Camille Desmoulins, 1793: 'They think gaining freedom is like growing up: you have to suffer.'
>
> Maximilien Robespierre, 1793: 'History is fiction.'

This passage marks a bridge between Mantel's invention of her characters' largely unknown youths and their increasingly public, increasingly iconic, brief adult lives.

I should like to say, in parenthesis, that the power of Mantel's and Barker's experimental third person narrations has something to do with the knowledgeable narrators they take from George Eliot. Fowles has said that the nineteenth-century narrator was assuming the omniscience of a god. I think rather the opposite is the case – this kind of fictive narrator can creep closer to the feelings and the inner life of characters – as well as providing a Greek chorus – than any first-person mimicry. In *Possession* I used this kind of narrator deliberately three times in the historical narrative – always to tell what the historians and biographers of my fiction never discovered, always to heighten the reader's imaginative entry into the world of the text. Barker and Mantel tell us what we can't know – they imagine it on the grand scale – and we are richer as readers.

Roberto Calasso, in *The Ruin of Kasch*, his extraordinary meditation on narration, storytelling, history, myth, has a wonderful quotation from Richard Cobb on the historian's interest precisely in the secret and the unknowable. Cobb describes his childhood desire to go into other people's houses, 'to get my foot in the door, to get behind the façade, to get inside. That, after all, is what being, or becoming, a historian is all about – the desire to read other peoples' letters, to breach privacy, to penetrate into the inner room.' Calasso compares this type of history to history as a collection of anecdotes of the Great. 'The true historian is the prime enemy of every hunter for the Memorable. His desired prey is primarily what has eluded memory and what has had every reason to elude it . . . At the end of his arrogant rise, the historian wants to meet Napoleon as if the latter were a stranger. At this point he becomes part visionary, and can muster the insolence to begin a book as Leon Bloy did: 'The history of Napoleon is surely the most unknown of all histories.'[19] Later he elaborates on secrecy in history in this way:

> The period between 1945 and the present could conceivably be rendered in two parallel histories: that of the historians with its elaborate apparatus of parameters, discussing figures, masses, parties, movements, negotiations, productions; and that of the secret service, telling of murders, traps, betrayals, assassinations, cover-ups and weapons shipments.

Secrecy, Calasso says, is post-History. He claims that the metaphysical meaning of the secret services lies in the words that designate them – 'they have violently forced secrecy to become apparent, too visible, as blatant as an advertisement posted on every corner. All secret services share a mission that is far more important and far more effective than all their conflicts: the annihilation of secrecy.'[20]

There is an interesting path to be explored here along the connections between modern historical novels and the popular genres that tell stories about secrecy, the spy story, the thriller, the detective novel. Calasso connects these modern stories of secrecy with earlier secret narratives.

> 'Hidden power' 'Secret organisation' 'Conspiracies' 'String pulling' 'Plot' 'Double dealing': these are words, mental gestures, that belong to gnosticism. At one time they were still illuminated by the oblique light of the Templars; today they designate murders, worldwide frauds, blackmail, abuses of power.[21]

Lawrence Norfolk's *Lemprière's Dictionary* looks very interesting in the light of these observations. It is a very long novel, set at the time of the French Revolution, at the heart of which is a conspiracy which is connected with a real secret organisation, a real plot, real double dealing, to do with the East India Company, the English funding of the resistance to the French Revolution, large shareholdings and the sieges of La Rochelle under Louis XIV and again under the Revolutionary state. Some of the fantastic events in Norfolk's fantastic novel are also described in Mantel's realist novel, and Schama's history. Complicity in the double dealing helped to bring down Danton, and fuelled the revolutionaries' predisposition and desire to see and invent conspiracies everywhere, royalist, religious, English, Austrian, bourgeois . . . Norfolk, like Mantel, claims that everything that seems improbable in his narrative is probably based on fact, and vice versa – what is plausible is invented. There are times when precise historical events do indeed seem improbable, unlikely, whereas it is the business of fictions, such as those nineteenth-century paradigms I quoted, to seem probable, representative of trends. Norfolk's Lemprière, the author of the real Classical Dictionary which inspired Keats, is hunting the source of mysteries about both his own ancestry and a series of mysterious deaths. His tale proceeds through incidents which parallel the events of his classical myths – his father is torn by dogs like Actaeon, a woman dies horribly of ingesting gold like Danaë. But these dreadful parallels are the plots, not of the novelist, but of conspirators in the novel. Nothing is what it seems but all is capable of explanation. Norfolk wanted originally to pattern his fiction so that it embodied all the scenes of the dictionary but fortunately had the sense to give up. His book is full of stories and brilliant details, and is a study of plot, layered fictiveness, organisation secret and fictional, the search for origins and the nature of riddles. It is a *tour de force* and completely different in intentions and form from Schama or Mantel.

So is my last example, also set at the turn of the eighteenth and nineteenth centuries, Penelope Fitzgerald's *The Blue Flower*. It has been suggested that postmodern historical novels seek out hidden, or unrecorded people and stories, often to tell the tales of the 'marginalised' – women, blacks, the colonised. Such stories, if written with political fervour, can be both powerful and uneasy – the correcting vision of the committed storyteller can create an unease in the less committed reader, who may feel persuaded or hectored – but in either case feels that the text has designs on him or her. Fitzgerald came late to writing historical novels – her early ones are set in contemporary Britain, and she did not begin writing novels until she was sixty. Her three most recent novels, *Innocence*, *The Beginning of Spring* and *The Blue Flower* extend her range, both in time and space. *Innocence*, most of which takes place in 1950s Italy, begins with a chilling and elegant account of a family of noble sixteenth-century Italians who were midgets, and whose daughter's companion, a dwarf, suddenly grows to normal height. The midget mistress, in her logical innocence, surrounded by her miniature world, sees this as a monstrous misfortune. She suggests that the girl be blinded and have her legs cut off at the knees. The way in which this coolly cruel, distant innocence reverberates in a modern Italian novel, the contrasts and similarities between the sixteenth-century Ridolfis and their twentieth-century descendants, Fitzgerald's economical depiction of a terrifying encounter with the dying Gramsci, of a dress designer from the thirties, and a modernising cleric, make this modern sharp comedy into a precise and idiosyncratic image of the history and thought of Italy.

This might be the moment to mention the Italian historical fiction of Jonathan Keates, a collection of stories, *Allegro Postillions* (1983), and *The Strangers' Gallery* (1987). Keates, who subsequently published a masterly biography of Stendhal, writes like Fitzgerald, at the edges of history. *The Strangers' Gallery* is set in 1847, just before the revolutions of 1848, as *The Beginning of Spring* is set just before the first world war and the Russian Revolution. Keates's tales have a tangential relation to real historical events, and his style, which is at ease with an elegant early nineteenth-century vocabulary nevertheless struck me, when I first met his work, as an extension of the possibilities of modern sentence structure and sensibility. He is an excellent example of the desire to set tales in the past in order to use a differently structured vocabulary and rhythm. His intelligence – and his human portraits – are those of an artist who understands the past by trying it on like a glove – but who is not writing either parody, or pastiche, or anything so simple as nostalgia.

Both *The Beginning of Spring* and *The Blue Flower*, as I said, are set at the edges of the great European revolutions. *The Beginning of Spring* is about an English printing firm in Moscow in 1913, just before both the Russian Revolution and the first world war. It is about private events in a world not yet overtaken by public events; it is an extraordinary, apparently simple, combining of Russian storytelling and English comedy; it creates a whole world of climate, city and landscape, machinery and habits of mind with minimal information. Fitzgerald notes novelist's details – cloth, smells, cigarettes, small deceits and sudden decisions, and makes an image of whole lives against a knowledge of historical crises to come. The precise odd date, 1913, makes the reader see this tale from two vantage-points. It is a moment when it is still possible to be involved in private fates, intricately and closely, with the sense that the characters are making personal, free decisions. Frank Reid's wife leaves him mysteriously at the beginning of the novel; he survives; at the end she returns of her own free will. But Fitzgerald's readers know that 1914 will change the private fates in a public way, and the public knowledge that the readers have and the characters have not – or have only a dim intimation of – creates a doubleness in the readers' sense of their own relation to the private tale. Historical novels know that their characters will die. They know what comes after. In *Innocence* Fitzgerald tells what comes after the beginning. In *The Beginning of Spring* she does not reveal anything, or discuss anything, of what comes after the end.

The Blue Flower is about a fairy tale without an end, written by the German Romantic poet, Fritz von Hardenberg, or Novalis. It is set in Saxony in the 1790s, after the French Revolution, and distant geographically from it – one of its pleasures is the depiction of the slow distances, the heavy earth, the difficulty and the sameness of German provincial society. Hardenberg was a Romantic poet, thinker and storyteller. He also worked in the salt-mines as an inspector. He was part of a large, vehement, impoverished noble family; his father was a Moravian Brother, with a strict protestant morality. He studied at Jena under Johann Gottlieb Fichte and was a friend of Friedrich Schlegel.

German Romantic ideas of infinity and timelessness provide one of the formal frames of Fitzgerald's tale, which is told in 55 very brief chapters, often only a page or two long. Early in the novel Fitzgerald quotes a letter from Schlegel, in which he describes 'a young man, from whom everything may be expected, and he explained himself to me at once with fire – with indescribably much fire . . . On the first evening he told me that the golden age would return, and that there was nothing evil in the world. I don't know if he is still of the same opinion.'[22] Hardenberg's politics were idealist but practical. Here (not included in Fitzgerald's novel) is a quotation from *Pollen*.

> Democracy, as it is commonly understood, is basically no different from monarchy, except that its monarch is a mass of heads. Authentic democracy is protestantism – a political state of nature, just as protestantism in the narrow sense is a religious state of nature.
>
> The moderate form of government is half state and half state of nature – it is an artificial and very fragile *machine* – and thus highly repulsive to all genial heads – but the hobby-horse of our time. Were this machine transformed into a living autonomous being, the major problem would be solved. The arbitrariness of nature and the compulsion of art penetrate each other when they are dissolved in spirit. Spirit liquefies both of them. Spirit is always poetic. The poetic state – is the true perfected state.[23]

Hardenberg called *Heinrich von Afterdingen* [sic] his '*political novel*' which 'would contain the apprenticeship of a *nation*'. (On the analogy of Wilhelm Meister.)

> The word *apprenticeship* is wrong – it expresses a certain *whither*. With me it should be nothing but – the *transition* from the infinite to the finite.[24]

Coleridge described the symbol as 'a putting of the infinite into the finite'. Hardenberg, arriving in the house of Karoline Just, sees the domestic objects transfigured, and embarrasses his hostess by crying out that it is all 'beautiful, beautiful'. Karoline's aunt (in Fitzgerald's novel) reproves him. 'You ought not to speak to Karoline quite like that. You did not mean it, and she is not used to it.'

> 'But I did mean it,' said Fritz. 'When I came into your home, everything, the wine-decanter, the tea, the sugar, the chairs, the dark green tablecloth with its abundant fringe, everything was illuminated.'
> 'They are as usual. I did not buy this furniture myself, but—'
> Fritz tried to explain that he had seen, not their everyday but their spiritual selves. He could not tell when these transfigurations would come to him. When the moment came it was as the whole world would be when body at last became subservient to soul.

Penelope Fitzgerald describes objects and incidents in the world of her fable of *The Blue Flower* with a precision and particularity which is at once part of Fritz's vision of infinite importance, and part of a comic, ironic novelist's vision of the awkward, sometimes terrible, human truths and finite moments and lives which Fritz's enthusiasm ignores. Her inexorable moral story shows Fritz's immediate vision of love for the twelve-year-old Sophie, its effect on his confidante Karoline which he is sublimely (and insensitively) unaware of, and the facts of Sophie's existence. She is ordinary, not bright, easily bored, she laughs a lot, and is afflicted with a tuberculosis of the liver which leads to horrible operations without anaesthetics, and death at fifteen. Before and after her death Fritz idealises her, punning on her name, into his 'Philosophy'. Largely through the dry, precise, responsible consciousnesses of her married sister, Frau Mandelsloh, and of Karoline, Fitzgerald offers an alternative image from infinite love of Wisdom – the single death of a not very interesting girl, at a terribly young age. Her moral lesson is one of attention to the particular, the lesson of George Eliot and Iris Murdoch – but Fitzgerald's particular includes Fritz's poetry, politics and visions as well as female wisdom, endurance, and irony.

At this point it is important to remember that all Fitzgerald's characters are historical persons, who lived and died. Fitzgerald has read and reread the five volumes of the Hardenberg correspondence and documents; she has studied the records of the salt-mines where Hardenberg worked. She has constructed her brief series of scenes and meditations as a very finite narrative concentration of something discursive and lengthy. The letters and documents were written by the living. Fitzgerald's web of quotation and fiction is both a brief resurrection and an imaginative vision of the dead, and their dead world. I wrote at the beginning of this essay of the aesthetic interest of the *unknowable* nature of the dead, of history. If a novelist invents a character, spins him or her out of her or himself and their reading, the character lives during the writing of the novel, and again during the reading, and dies with the novel. '*Madame Bovary, c'est moi*' and Anna Karenina was Tolstoy, and their authors killed them. Something different is going on in *The Blue Flower*, as it was in Anthony Burgess's resurrection of Keats, in order to relive, to infiltrate, the myth of his death. Simon Schama has said that he felt, writing about the lives and deaths of individuals in *Citizens*, that he was in some sense bringing them to life again, and they would die again when he took his attention away from them. (Like Odysseus filling the Shades with living blood so that they might speak.)

The epigraph to Fitzgerald's *The Blue Flower* is a saying of Novalis, or Hardenberg. 'Novels arise out of the shortcomings of history.' Fitzgerald patterns her novel with Hardenberg's assertions about poetry and politics and history. Hardenberg's host says to him

> 'The Revolution in France has not produced the effects once hoped for . . . It has not resulted in a golden age.'

'No, they've made a butcher's shop of it, I grant you that,' said Fritz. 'But the spirit of the Revolution, as we first heard of it, as it first came to us, could be preserved here in Germany. It could be transferred to the world of the imagination and administered by poets.'

The Kreisamtmann goes on to discuss the Dutch philosopher Hemsterhuis's idea that there was once a universal language of plants, stars and stones, and man.

'For example the sun communicates with the stone as it warms it. Once we knew the words of this language, and we shall do so again, since history always repeats itself . . .'

Fritz, comforting himself for Sophie's illness writes, 'Algebra, like laudanum, deadens pain,' and goes on to speak of his glimpses of 'a totally different system' behind the laws that govern our existence. He remembers his vision of the Justs' house and 'the certainty of immortality, like the touch of a hand'.

As things are, we are the enemies of the world, and foreigners to this earth. Our grasp of it is a process of estrangement. Through estrangement itself I earn my living from day to day. I say, this is animate, but that is inanimate. I am a salt Inspector, this is rock salt. I go further than this, much further, and say this is waking, this is a dream, this belongs to the body, that to the spirit, this belongs to space and distance, that to time and duration. But space spills over into time as the body into the soul . . .'

Many of the historical novels I have so far discussed have found it necessary to contain images, riddling, dubious, or like Burgess's ideal sonnet form, durable, of the immortal and the infinite. But Fitzgerald is, I think, a Parmenidean novelist. She will give us images of time's cycle, of restoration and spirit. For Novalis, the novel which took over from the shortcomings of history was his ideal tale, his political novel, *Heinrich von Afterdingen*, containing the open-ended fairy tale of the lost blue flower. But Fitzgerald the historical novelist knows about irredeemable time. At the beginning of her novel she resurrects

Hardenberg's young brother, der Bernhard, full of intelligence and revolutionary enthusiasm, with his red revolutionary cap. At the beginning of the novel Fritz saves der Bernhard from drowning. After its close Fitzgerald gives a catalogue of the rapid young deaths of Fritz and his siblings, mostly from tuberculosis. Der Bernhard, she says, was drowned in 1800. Time, as Wallace Stevens says, will not relent.

· 3 ·

Ancestors

I have talked about the novel of recent memory, and the relations between fiction and history. I now want to look at the effects on the forms of fiction of the ideas we loosely call Darwinian, although they owe as much to the geologists, like Lyell, and sociological thinkers like Herbert Spencer. I have suggested that the stories we tell about ourselves take form from the large paradigmatic narratives we inhabit. Human lives used to be thought out in terms of the Biblical narrative. Related narratives were made of the significance of lives – the allegory of Everyman, of *Pilgrim's Progress*, the saints' lives and Confessions against which the Bildungsroman formed itself in turn. Alternative forms are the national epic, from Virgil to the Comédie Humaine. (Before and after those are fairy tales and philosophical tales.) In the nineteenth century, as Stephen Jay Gould has shown in *Time's Arrow, Time's Cycle*, the discovery of 'deep time' shook concepts of history, of the purpose and significance (if there was any) of individual lives. At the same time Darwin's patient experiments on adaptations, selection, inheritance, created a very different narrative of human origins – and by implication, of human destiny – from the Biblical one of creation, salvation, and resurrection. The early utopian enthusiasts for Social Darwinism brought much of this thinking into uneasy disrepute. The discovery and study of the function of DNA introduced a new wave of Darwinism, which moved out into ethics and indeed politics, with books like Richard Dawkins's *The Selfish Gene* and later studies like Matt Ridley's *Altruism*. It seems inevitable that such profound changes in our sense of the nature of time and the nature of human relations should give rise to changes in the forms, as well as the subjects, of fiction. This essay looks at some of them. History is neither the working-out of the divine plan, nor simply the history of political progress and destruction. A new kind of historical novel might be possible. The process of adaptation, as Darwin said, is slow and gradual, and much current fiction springs out of a resistance to the implications of his ideas – a resistance sometimes nostalgic, sometimes combative.

George Eliot was perhaps the English novelist whose interest in the new forms of thought had the most complex effect on the forms of her own writing. She saw her novels, I think, as 'natural histories' – I take the term from her admiring essay on Riehl's *Natural History of German Life*. She said famously of *Middlemarch* and its artistic coherence 'nothing will be seen to be irrelevant to my design, which is to show the gradual action of ordinary causes rather than exceptional'.[1] This phrase suggests the work in deep time of both Lyell's geological changes and Darwin's adaptations. In a novel like *The Mill on the Floss* she sees the human community in terms of the development of natural forms through deep time – the village of St Ogg's is 'a continuation and outgrowth of nature . . . which carries the traces of its long growth and history like a millennial tree'. In her 'Ilfracombe Journal' she observes human habitations with a Darwinian naturalist's eye.

> In hilly districts, where houses and clusters of houses look so tiny against the huge limbs of Mother Earth, one cannot help thinking of man as a parasitic animal – an epizoon making his abode on the skin of the planetary organism. In a flat country a house or a town looks imposing – there is nothing to rival it in height, and we may imagine the earth a mere pedestal for us. But when one sees a house stuck on the side of a great hill, and still more a number of houses looking like a few barnacles clustered on the side of a great rock, we begin to think of the strong family likenesses between ourselves and all other building, burrowing, house-appropriating and shell-secreting animals. The difference between a man with his house and a mollusc with its shell lies in the number of steps and

phenomena interposed between the fact of individual existence and the completion of the building.[2]

To simplify fiercely – George Eliot's natural histories insist on the gradual operation of natural laws, which is her image of time, and the comparison, and relation, of human beings to the creatures, in a way quite different from Swift's savagely satirical comparisons in *Gulliver's Travels*, or for that matter Pope's careful distinction between creatures and humans in the *Essay on Man*, with its microscopic-eyed fly, and spider with exquisite touch, all in their place in an order on a ladder. Eliot sensed what DNA shows – that all living forms are quite closely related.

Recent British novels, too, have been interested in the history of the creatures as part of our natural history. Lawrence Norfolk's *The Pope's Rhinoceros* is nearly 800 pages of extravagant narrative, set in the Baltic, Renaissance Rome and the African rainforest. It tells of conspiracies, religious wars, a plague of super-rats, monks, soldiers, and the desire of the Pope for the fabulous beast, drawn from imagination by Dürer, correlated with the unicorn, named only in the title. One of Norfolk's starting-points was Ionesco's surreal *Rhinoceros*. His text is full of postmodern quotations from later, indeed contemporary, texts, but it has a narrative energy that derives from his admiration of Dumas. Nevertheless it is a Darwinian tale, with a concisely Darwinian epigraph from Arne Lindroth.

All fishes eat. All fishes spawn. Few fishes spawn where they eat.

Norfolk's novel opens with a long, wonderfully written account of the formation of the Baltic in deep time, where in due course it becomes clear that the central consciousness, the reader's point-of-view, is or are the herring shoals. I can't quote it all – here are a few stray sentences to give an idea:

This sea was once a lake of ice. High mountains overlooked a glacial plain frosted with snow and scoured by the freezing wind. Granite basins curved up from under the ice tonnage to rim it with irregular coasts. In ages still to come, boulder waste and till will speak of the ice pack's tortuous inching over buried rock and sandstone; moraines and drumlins of advances and recessions that gouge out trenches and shunt forward ridges. The sea floor here was prepared long before there was a sea to cover it. In the interim came the governance of ice . . .

This surface interruption: a pale disc of light germinating in the snow-flecked sky suggests a radical tilt to the axis below, gales cede to gusts and vicious whirlwinds, ice giants shout in the night. An inch of silt marks a thousand years, an aeon means a single degree of arc and by this scale a thaw is under-way. There will be a century of centuries of snarling ice . . .[3]

The creatures proliferate and are named, not Adamically, but scientifically and poetically.

The first men never returned. Peat bogs, beech scrub, and moorland lay undisturbed for centuries while fish entered by the belts, spawned in the brackish waters, grew fat on sea snails, brown shrimps, bristle worms and soft-shelled crabs. Atlantic salmon sped east with the sea trout and grayling to spawn in the great rivers whose mouths in summer would choke with the bodies of spent lampreys until shrieking gulls and goosanders plucked them from the water. Flounder, dab, sand-eels and lumpsuckers grazed the saline bottom waters while gudgeon, pike and dace hovered about the freshwater outflows. Cod spawned in Arkona Deep, grew huge, ate each other. The spring and autumn herring founded their colonies in the nearby shallows off the islands of Rügen and Usedom. A million undisturbed existences floated, swam, spawned, and died before the first keel cut the waves above and the nets descended to haul the sea's fat harvest ashore. Invasions, battles and slaughter were a vague clangour, dim thuds in the deathly air; the pale bodies sank quietly watched by lidless, curious eyes.

Close reading of this could look at the ambivalent human metaphors used for the creatures – the herrings 'founding their colonies' for example, and the insertion of words from the word-hoard of Scandinavian sagas and songs. The effect is double – to diminish the importance of human events, and at the same time to create a paradisal nostalgia (there are Miltonic echoes also) for the plenitude of a natural world unpolluted by humans. If the war novels of the post-war generation are haunted by fear of the promised End of nuclear war, this younger generation is afraid of the destruction of biodiversity, of huge parts of the solid and watery earth. We see the earth as a connected web of lives and environments in part because of the rapidity of communications, and we fear for its destruction, the tearing of huge rents in the web. It is no accident that *The Pope's Rhinoceros* is set in both icy seas and tropical rainforests, and that its action is about greed and slaughter. Our imaginations inhabit these things and also these places. Owing to technology we have *seen* the icy depths and the sweltering jungle. We are part of it, and we are destroying it.

I wrote in previous essays about Graham Swift's *Waterland*[4] and Julian Barnes's *A History of the World in 10½ Chapters* in terms of their riddling narrative experiments with history and storytelling. It is worth pointing out that both are also 'natural histories'. Consider some chapter headings in *Waterland*.

> QUATORZE JUILLET
> CHILD'S PLAY
> FORGET THE BASTILLE
> ABOUT THE EEL
> ABOUT NATURAL HISTORY
> AND ARTIFICIAL HISTORY

'Quatorze Juillet' tells of the fall of the Bastille in one mocking and deflating page; 'Child's Play' describes fen children playing sex games on 14 July 1940 under threat of invasion from Hitler, with an eel in Mary's knickers; 'Forget the Bastille' compares historical curiosity with sexual and more primitive curiosity. Swift praises the curiosity of humble historians which he associates with the perennial curiosity of scientists and explorers, asking rhetorically whether his reader has ever wondered whether so many political movements – not only the revolutionary ones, fail. He suggests that it is perhaps because these movements fail to allow for the unpredictable and complicated expressions of human curiosity.

There follows the chapter, 'About the Eel' – the best, the most imaginative, the most surprising chapter in a book where the human characters, perhaps intentionally, are banal. It tells of the researches of Linnaeus and Johannes Schmidt, Danish oceanographer and ichthyologist, who set out to discover the breeding ground of the European eel. It tells of myths, legends, wrong opinions about the breeding cycle and migrations to and from the Sargasso Sea of the European eel, the riddle of whose sex-life and birth remains unsolved. It sets cycles and migrations against linear History. The next chapter, 'About Natural History', defines Natural History as something which doesn't go anywhere, adheres to itself, and continually returns to its source. And Swift's arch narrator, nevertheless speaking for Swift, speaks in praise of the mystery of human nature, and 'love of life'. He rhapsodises about natural history and human nature, claiming that the 'natural stuff' is always overcoming the artificial stuff, and telling the children that our love of life is more seditious, and more anarchic, than any Tennis-Court Oath. Revolutions he says, smell of the death-wish, and Terror is always lurking round the corner.

To be meaningful, this argument has to be set against the politicised feel of 1970s literature, theory and criticism. It sets biology against cultural theory and claims – with the use of a lot of words from that romanticism which T.E. Hulme called 'spilt religion' – 'mystery of mysteries', 'unfathomable' – that the one is more complex and fundamental than the other. I am uneasy about this unthinking romantic core in the middle of all Swift's fiction. It is all too easy for novels to be mockingly, or sentimentally, or both, on the side of 'life'. It's a case of 'By God you'd better,' as someone said of Carlyle's acceptance of the Universe. But the next chapter, which is called 'And Artificial History' is a delicious piece of intertextual layering, as the adolescent hero, during the Battle of Britain, reads Charles Kingsley's historical novel, *Hereward the Wake*, mixing magic, fairy-tale chronicle and history, about the last stand of an Englishman in the fens during an invasion from Normandy. Swift uses a metaphor of white scrolls for the sky-traces of the Battle of Britain, the stuff of future legends, and his narrator asks rhetorically who can now say that history doesn't go in circles.

Next to Norfolk's herring and Swift's eels, let us briefly reconsider Barnes's woodworm. Its account of the voyage of the Ark is farcical and whimsical, but it does present the human myth of responsibility to and for the creatures as untrue. 'It wasn't a nature reserve, that Ark of ours; at times it was more like a prison ship.'

> Now I realise that accounts differ. Your species has its much repeated version, which still charms even sceptics; while the animals have a compendium of sentimental myths. But they're not going to rock the boat, are they? Not when they've been treated as heroes, not when it's become a matter of pride that each and every one of them can trace its family tree straight back to the Ark. They were chosen, they endured, they survived . . . I was never chosen. In fact, like several other species, I was specifically not chosen. I was a stowaway; I too survived; I escaped (getting off was no easier than getting on) and I have flourished.

This creature is later tried for sacrilege, heard tapping in woodwork as an omen of human death or simply advertising its own sexuality. It infests picture-frames and may destroy great works of art. Its tale is the ironic counterpoint to the Biblical parody, the natural history of survival that isn't human, and gives the reader a different viewpoint. This novel too has its humans lost in the rainforest, its animals (irradiated reindeer) innocent victims of human incompetence or folly. It too ends up with a romantic vision of human love to set against a reductive view of human importance:

> The materialist argument attacks love of course; it attacks everything. Love boils down to pheromones, it says. This bounding of the heart, this clarity of vision, this energizing, this moral certainty, this exaltation, this civic virtue, this murmured *I love you*, are all caused by a low-level smell emitted by one partner and subconsciously nosed by another. We are just a grander version of that beetle bashing its head in a box at the sound of a tapped pencil. Do we believe this? Well,

let's believe it for a moment, because it makes love's triumph the greater. What is a violin made of? Bits of wood and bits of sheep's intestine. Does its construction demean and banalise music? On the contrary, it exalts the music further.[5]

A number of British historical novels have been written in the last thirty years which are either set in the Victorian period, or partly in the Victorian and partly in the modern periods. In several of these Darwin is either a character, or a present voice. Jenny Diski's *The Monkey's Uncle*, for instance, describes the breakdown of Charlotte FitzRoy, a fictive modern relation of Captain FitzRoy of the *Beagle*. Charlotte and a female orang-utan in a wonderland like Alice's meet Marx, Freud, and Darwin. Roger McDonald's *Mr Darwin's Shooter* (1998) tells the story of Syms Covington, servant to Charles Darwin on the *Beagle*. Liz Jensen's *Ark* is set partly in a future where human fertility has failed and pets have replaced children, partly in a past where exotic animals were hunted and stuffed for Queen Victoria's pleasure.

In several of these novels are references both to Philip Gosse, who believed against all the evidence that God had planted the fossils in the crust of the earth to mislead humans, and to Mary Anning, who discovered a large number of fossil creatures, including the first *Ichthyosaurus platydon*, at Lyme Regis. A regular *topos*, almost a cliché in these novels is the Victorian hero's encounter with a fossilised creature, representing deep time. These descriptions perhaps originate in Thomas Hardy's *A Pair of Blue Eyes* (1873) where Henry Knight, having fallen over a cliff, finds himself suspended face to face with a trilobite.

> It was a creature with eyes. The eyes, dead and turned to stone, were even now regarding him. Separated by millions of years in their lives, Knight and this underling seemed to have met in their place of death . . .
>
> Knight was a fair geologist; and such is the supremacy of habit over occasion, as a pioneer of the thoughts of men, that at this dreadful juncture his mind found time to take in, by a momentary sweep, the varied scenes between this creature's epoch and his own.

Time closed up like a fan before him. He saw himself at one extremity of the years, face to face with the beginning and all the intermediate centuries simultaneously. Fierce men, clothed in the hides of beasts, and carrying, for defence and attack, huge clubs and pointed spears, rose from the rock, like phantoms before the doomed Macbeth . . . behind them stood an earlier band. No man was there. Huge elephantine forms, the mastodon, the hippopotamus, the tapir, antelopes of monstrous size, the megatherium, and the myledon – all for the moment in juxtaposition. Further back and overlapped by these, were perched huge-billed birds and swinish creatures as large as horses. Still more shadowy were the sinister crocodilian outlines – alligators and other uncouth shapes, culminating in the colossal lizard, the iguanodon. Folded behind were dragon forms and clouds of flying reptiles: still underneath were fishy beings of lower development; and so on, till the lifetime scenes of the fossil confronting him were a present and modern condition of things.[6]

Hardy's character hangs on, brooding on nature personified as 'a person with a curious temper; as one who does not scatter kindnesses and cruelties alternately, impartially and in order, but heartless severities or overwhelming generosities in lawless caprice'. This is the opposite of George Eliot's sense of the inexorable forms of natural law – I shall come back to the opposition of probability and chance, both as subject and as form of the novel later. Hardy's blindly staring fossil has many descendants. Graham Swift's modern hero, in *Ever After*, has a safe niche at a Cambridge college, where he is editing the notebooks of a Victorian ancestor of his own. The ancestor, Matthew, fails to rescue a damsel in distress (with a twisted ankle) in Lyme Regis and meets an ichthyosaur. He leaves the path of romance and *Persuasion* and ascends the path of development and evolution. This causes him to lose his faith, and eventually his happy marriage, and his work as an engineer with Brunel. The Victorian calls the moment of his unbelief the beginning of his make-believe. The modern man, for whom ichthyosaurs are commonplace, cannot quite manage to write convincingly of the shock, the new vision of time and self. He sees the buried, unimaginably ancient skull as 'the thing itself'.

In *A Change of Climate*, a much more modern novel starting in 1970 but reaching back to the second world war, Hilary Mantel's hero, Ralph, finds a 150-million year old fossil, *Gryphaeus*, which is known as the 'Devil's Toenail' – it has a 'thick ridged ogreish curve, a greenish sinister sheen'. He has visions, The visions correspond with those of Hardy and Swift.

> A frieze of evolution marched through Ralph's head. Each form of life has its time and place: sea-snail and sea-lily, water-scorpion and lungfish, fern tree and coral. Shark and flesh-eating reptile; sea-urchin and brontosaurus; pterodactyl and magnolia tree; cuttle fish and oyster. Then the giant flightless bird, opossum in his tree, elephant in his swamp; it was as clear in his mind as it might be in a child's picture book, or a poster on a nursery wall. The sabre-toothed cat, the little horse three feet tall; the Irish elk, the woolly mammoth; then man, stooped, hairy, furrow-browed. It is a success story.
>
> At seventeen Ralph could be taken for a man, but not of this primitive textbook kind. He was tall, strong, with a clear skin and clear eyes, like a hero in a slushy book.[8]

He wants to become a geologist, but is blackmailed by his religious parents (from a backward-looking sect, jokingly known as the East Anglia fossils) into becoming a missionary in Africa. There, he experiences evil – one of the best descriptions of real evil, a heart of darkness, I've ever read – which reaches into his future, destroying goodwill and love. Mantel's epigraphs are also interesting.

> Charles Darwin, *The Descent of Man*, 1871: 'We are not here concerned with hopes and fears, only with the truth as far as our reason allows us to discover it. I have given the evidence to the best of my ability.'

Job 4:7 'Consider, what innocent ever perished, or where have the righteous been destroyed?'

At the end Ralph jettisons the fossil.

His hand crept into the first drawer of his desk. Closed around stone. Gryphaea. He held it to his cheek, and then against his mouth. A child's life; the salt and cold. He tasted it. Phylum: Mollusca. Class:Pelecypoda. Order: Pterioda. Such confidence, he'd felt as a child, about the order of the world. Family: Gryphaeidae. Genus: *Gryphaea*. Species: *arcuata*. The past doesn't change, of course: it lies behind you, petrified, immutable. What changes it is the way you see it. Perception is everything. It turns villains into heroes and victims into collaborators. He held the object up between his fingers: took a sighting, and spun it across the room into the wastepaper basket.

Phylum, Class, Order, Family, Genus, Species. These are the categories of Linnaeus's *Scala Naturae*, and Linnaeus is much mocked in modern evolutionary fictions. John Fowles's hero in *The French Lieutenant's Woman* has his encounter with fossils also on Lyme Beach, where he looks for 'tests', fossil echinoderms or sea-urchins. Fowles writes as a knowing modern about both his hero and Darwin.

Charles called himself a Darwinist, and yet he had not really understood Darwin. But then, nor had Darwin himself. What that genius had upset was the Linnaean *Scala Naturae*, the ladder of nature, whose great keystone, as essential to it as the divinity of Christ to theology, was *nulla species nova*: a new species cannot enter the world. This principle explains the Linnaean obsession with classifying and naming, with fossilizing the existent. We can see it now as a fore-doomed attempt to stabilise and fix what is in reality a continuous flux, and it seems highly appropriate that Linnaeus himself finally went mad; he knew he was in a labyrinth but not that it was one whose walls and passages were eternally changing. Even Darwin never quite shook off the Swedish fetters . . .[9]

Fowles's Charles stares at the lias strata in the cliff and – failing to realise the idea of general extinction of species – finds in them

> an immensely reassuring orderliness in existence. He might perhaps have seen a very contemporary social symbolism in the way those grey-blue ledges were crumbling; but what he did see was a kind of edificiality of time, in which inexorable laws (therefore beneficently divine, for who could argue that order was not the highest human good?) very conveniently arranged themselves for the survival of the fittest and the best, *exempli gratia* Charles Smithson, this fine spring day, alone, eager and inquiring, understanding, accepting, noting and grateful.

Charles is tested by his attraction to Sarah, the sexually tempting French Lieutenant's Woman. He sees his rejection of her as a hysteric as an exercise of his reasonable free will, and his inability to keep up this reasonable vision as a loss of free will to the point where he has 'no more freewill than an ammonite'. Fowles's views on Victorian fears of sensuality and sexuality are bound up in his own 1960s commitment to existentialism and the 'moment of vision'. Fowles's narrative voice in this novel is, according to him, a parody of the knowing third-person voice of the high Victorian novel – though his didactic and superior attitude to his Victorians has more than a touch of Lytton Strachey's Bloomsbury deflation for the sake of deflation. Sarah's 'real nature' this narrator tells us is sensuous.

> To most Englishmen of his age such an intuition of Sarah's real nature would have been repellent; and it did very faintly repel – or at least shock – Charles. He shared enough of his contemporaries' prejudices to suspect sensuality in any form; but whereas they would, by one of those terrible equations that take place at the behest of the super-ego, have made Sarah vaguely responsible for being born as she was, he did not. For that we can thank his scientific hobbies. Darwinism, as its shrewder opponents realised, let open the floodgates to something more serious than the undermining of the Biblical

account of the origins of man; its deepest implications lay in the direction of determinism and behaviourism, that is, towards philosophies that reduce morality to a hypocrisy and duty to a straw hat in a hurricane.

I want to digress – apparently – for a moment – to quote Fowles's description of Charles's vision of the living creatures (his eels, his herring, his worms). In his case it is a wood full of birds, and, importantly, one individual bird. It is set up with a mixture of scientific and religious language. 'It seemed strangely distinct, this undefiled dawn sun. It had almost a smell, as of warm stone, a sharp dust of photons streaming down through space.' The ashes and sycamores 'erected their dewy vaults of young leaves; there was something mysteriously religious about them, but of a religion before religion; a druid balm, a green sweetness over all . . .' Fowles (not his hero) compares the scene to a painting by Pisanello of St Hubert in an early Renaissance forest 'confronted by birds and beasts. The saint is shocked, almost as if the victim of a practical joke, all his arrogance dowsed by a sudden drench of nature's profoundest secret: the universal parity of existence'. There follows a list of named singing birds 'blackcaps, whitethroats, thrushes, blackbirds, wood-pigeons . . .' Charles experiences each as unique and perfect, in 'an exquisitely particular universe, in which each was appointed, each unique'.

> A tiny wren perched on top of a bramble not ten feet from him and trilled its violent song. He saw its glittering black eyes, the red and yellow of its song-gaped throat – a midget ball of feathers that yet managed to make itself the Announcing Angel of evolution: I am what I am, thou shalt not pass my being now . . .
>
> It seemed to announce a far deeper and stranger reality than the pseudo-Linnaean one that Charles had sensed on the beach that earlier morning – perhaps nothing more original than a priority of existence over death, of the individual over the species, of ecology over classification. We take such priorities for granted today.

Charles later compares Sarah and her wildness to the wren. Fowles uses the occasion for an existentialist sermon.

> There was a wildness about her. Not the wildness of lunacy or hysteria – but that same wildness Charles had sensed in the wren's singing . . . a wildness of innocence, almost of eagerness . . .

The immediacy of Sarah's face confounds his theories of clinical horrors.

> In spite of Hegel, the Victorians were not a dialectically minded age; they did not think naturally in opposites, of positives and negatives as aspects of the same whole. Paradoxes troubled rather than pleased them. They were not people for existentialist moments, but for chains of cause and effect; for positive all-explaining theories, carefully studied and studiously applied. They were busy erecting of course; and we have been busy demolishing for so long that now erection seems as ephemeral an activity as bubble-blowing.

Fowles's novel was one of the first of what is almost a genre, that Sally Shuttleworth defines as 'the retro-Victorian novel' in an essay that compares my own *Possession* and *Angels and Insects* with Graham Swift's *Ever After*. She sees a kind of nostalgic desire for crisis, for the drama of loss of faith, as a driving force in the writing of such novels.[10]

> Perhaps this is the ultimate key to the current nostalgia for the Victorian era. For the Victorians there was a decisive crisis of faith, a sense that the world was shaking under them, an ecstatic agony of indecision. For the post-modern era no such form of crisis seems possible, for there are no fixed boundaries of belief. It is an age of 'ontological doubt' without any fixed point of faith against which to define itself. Many of the retro-Victorian texts are informed by a sense of loss, but it is a *second order* loss. It is not loss of a specific belief system, but rather the loss of that sense of immediacy and urgency which comes with true existential crisis.

It seems odd, in a way, to write natural histories, centring on a set of beliefs in gradual change, minute adaptations over long, almost immeasurable periods of time, and to construct them around the existential moment of a crisis of faith. My own intentions, as I recollect them, were more to do with rescuing the complicated Victorian thinkers from modern diminishing parodies like those of Fowles and Lytton Strachey, and from the disparaging mockery (especially of the poets) of Leavis and T.S. Eliot. 'Tennyson and Browning were poets and they thought; but they did not feel their thought as immediately as the odour of a rose.'[11] Nonsense – but my generation believed it.

I have also a concern, as will be clear from these essays, with the relations between religious thought and narratives and narrative works of art. I was much impressed, as a young writer, by Iris Murdoch's understanding of the effect on the moral life – and therefore on fiction – of a true understanding of the removal of a divine source of morals and a transcendent sanction of behaviour. I was struck by Grahame Greene's assertion that with the death of Henry James 'the religious sense was lost to the English novel, and with the religious sense went the sense of the importance of the human act'. The characters of Woolf and Forster, Greene said, 'wandered like cardboard symbols through a world that was paper-thin'.[12] I don't think this concern is the same as a nostalgia for existential crisis – indeed I am happy enough in a world where the curiosity praised by the *Waterland* chapter on Natural History is an important value, and I write about scientists because they do not spend their time deconstructing the world, or quibbling theologically about abstract terms of value. I am interested in the Natural History of religion – unlike many of the Darwinian scientists I meet who are pugnaciously opposed to any interest in this ancient and complex form of human behaviour. My clergyman in *Morpho Eugenia* is trying to believe in both Darwin and the Church, as Charles Kingsley did, and the Duke of Argyll, and many other clergymen naturalists. But my hero is the Amazonian naturalist, based on Bates and Wallace.

The companion piece, *The Conjugial Angel*, is a study of Tennyson's doubt and his family's Swedenborgian spiritualism, faced with death – table-rapping was seen as a natural religion for a 'materialist age'. Like the spiritualist material in *Possession* it has its roots in my work on the James family – the elder Henry, who 'wrote *The Secret of Swedenborg* and kept it', William James, psychologist, pragmatist and author of possibly the greatest scientific study of religion, *The Varieties of Religious Experience*, and Henry James the novelist, author of *The Bostonians* which chronicles the extraordinary nineteenth-century intellectual and social melting-pot where feminism, utopianism, spiritualism, transcendentalism, Fourierism and ideas of harmony are wildly entwined. The nineteenth-century spiritualists claimed the metallurgist and visionary, Emanuel Swedenborg as a founding father. Modern spiritualist texts strangely stress their 'scientific' superiority to more traditional religions. All this illuminates *In Memoriam*, which I believe to be one of the greatest poems in English, or in any language, and which embodies religious doubt in the face of individual death with fears of natural chance, necessity and transmutation derived from science that preceded Darwin.

The tradition of comparing insect and human societies also precedes the work of Darwin and the socio-biologists. I began thinking about insects very young, long before I had read E.O.Wilson's books on ants, when Wilson himself was discovering pheromones. I began with an instinctive aversion to anthropomorphic personifications – Maeterlinck's Queen Ant in her bridal veiling, committing infanticide, or whimsical parallels between insect armies, rulers and 'servants' with human hierarchies. I worry about anthropomorphism as a form of self-deception. (The Christian religion is an anthropomorphic account of the universe.) Recent discoveries about the great extent to which DNA patterns are shared by all creatures have perhaps changed writers' ideas of the natural world, and have certainly modified my choice of difference as the important thing to look at. There are true links to be made between species, even beyond the morphological links made by Cuvier and his followers. One of the things that delighted me about writing *Angels and Insects* was playing with the comparison of human ideals of beauty (in the Victorian age) and beauty in the creatures.

The early evolutionary thinkers were baffled by the beauty of male birds and butterflies, and showed a male tendency at first to think of this as merely a sign of the greater importance of that sex. Then both Wallace and Darwin began to think about the idea of sexual selection, of female choice. Darwinian ideas affected two kinds of narrative that were venerable parts of the forms of Western art. They affected not only the idea of religion – creation, salvation, immortality – but the quite different idea of romantic love. This idea had been undercut by the 'scientific' novels, from *Wahlverwandtschaften* to *Madame Bovary*. Gillian Beer has pointed out that George Eliot, in the opening scene of *Daniel Deronda*, is using Darwinian ideas both of natural and sexual selection.[13] Gwendolen is playing games of chance in an obsessive way – which turns out to be her only recourse, literally and metaphorically, in the battle for survival, and an inadequate one. The question is asked 'Was she beautiful?' and the asker is later revealed to be Daniel Deronda, who does not come to love Gwendolen, but whose question betrays his interest in her as a woman. I wanted in *Morpho Eugenia* to depict my hero's passionate attraction to the beautiful and well-bred Eugenia Alabaster as a question of pheromones and Victorian romantic love combined – disastrously. I was also playing with ideas going back to Walter Scott of Englishness and Normanness, as they appear in *Ivanhoe*. The Alabasters are the Anglo-Saxons. William, son of a Yorkshire butcher, is called Adamson – because like Linnaeus, he named the unknown insects in the tropics. But he is also, being the 'new man', the scientist, William the Conqueror, and sets off for the rainforest with Matty – Matilda – the predatory worker-turned-queen in the metaphorical anthill. It's a quiet image of shifting class and sexual hierarchies, too – both Wallace and Bates were explorers from modest backgrounds, who travelled not in the British Empire, but in the unknown Amazon, for reasons of pure curiosity.

I have already remarked on the half-chapter in praise of romantic love in *A History of the World in 10½ Chapters*. This compares in an interesting way to two novels by Graham Swift and Ian McEwan. Their titles – *Ever After* and *Enduring Love* – are suggestive. I have already talked about the 'Darwinian' content of *Ever After* in terms of the nineteenth-century crisis of faith. The modern plot of the book concerns the narrator – who describes himself in the first sentence as a dead man. He has tried to kill himself out of despair over the death of his wife Ruth, a famous actress who killed herself to save herself from the last stages of lung cancer. His father previously committed suicide – it is suggested because his mother left him for a cheerful rich American, owner of a plastic empire, but in 'fact' it turns out in despair at the prospect of the atomic bomb. The modern story is loaded with death. But it is also a genuine love story – which works in its simplicity – the narrator is quite convincing in his depiction of death-surrounded romantic passion for a woman who is both a real woman and endlessly versatile at shape-shifting into other lives and forms. Much of the force of the love which is set against death derives from a metaphor of burning. The narrator returns frequently to a metaphor of people as combustible fuel – some burn more brightly, some less, but all move from fuel to fire to ash. This metaphor of the burning of energy is connected both to Brunel, with his perpetual cigar, in the nineteenth-century story, and to Ruth, a chain-smoker, in the modern one. They are then connected to Ruth's performance of the great romantic lover, Cleopatra, burning in her suicide – 'I am fire and air – my other elements/I give to baser life.' It is Cleopatra who has many of the best lines about the infinity of romantic love. 'Eternity was in our lips and eyes/Bliss in our brows bent.' 'I have/Immortal longings in me.' At the end of his novel Swift describes the first time the narrator and Ruth make love – the ordinariness, the specific bliss. The narrator tells his lover what he had told no one – that his father 'took his own life'. Swift repeats the phrase, remarking that it appears impossible that the two young lovers who appear to have lived, and loved, so intensely that night, will ever come to this point. The novel ends on a repetition of the phrase, he took his life.

In this context, the narrator is 'taking his life' by coming alive in love. The father, exactly opposite, takes his life by destroying it. Both are individual acts, as Ruth's voluntary suicide will be. The romantic love is the image of immortality in the midst of linear history, of the

story of life and death which is all natural history. *Ever After* –
without the 'Happy' – is and is not an ironic title, a simulacrum of the
storyteller's false infinity at the end of the fairy tale.

Enduring Love also mixes Darwinian and romantic messages. It is not
a historical novel, and is far too intricate to describe adequately in this
context. It opens with a scene in which a group of people try to prevent
a capsized balloon from setting off again – they do not all pull together,
and the most altruistic, who hangs on longest, is killed. One of the
rescuers, Jed, has a moment of vision in which he realises that it is his
destiny to love the narrator – this destiny is a fantasy, with both
religious and erotic components. It ruins the powerful and well-
founded love of the narrator and his wife. The narrator is a scientific
journalist – he is working, amongst other things, on the narratives, the
anecdotes, of Darwinian history. His wife is a Keats scholar, and is
working on romantic love in a quite different context. In an extraordinary scene in a restaurant, on the birthday of Clarissa, the Keats
scholar, she receives two presents. One, from her godfather, who 'had
been appointed to an honorary position on the Human Genome
project' is a gold brooch, in the double spiral form of DNA. One, from
the narrator, her husband, is a first edition of Keats's first collection,
Poems (1817). They discuss Wordsworth's arrogance to Keats. At this
point two gunmen, hired by Jed, approach their table and shoot – by
pure accident – a complete stranger at the next table. Later, the
narrator, trying to recall the incident remembers a sentence. 'By then,
Keats was dead.'

Enduring Love is in some ways more interesting than *Ever After*, since
it juxtaposes a mad version of the plottedness of human relations, the
divine design, the instant recognition of the beloved and destiny, with
a human love which is vulnerable, can be destroyed by madness and
certainty. It has its own image of the creatures and deep time, seen at
the moment when the narrator goes to shit in a wood after buying a
gun.

> Some people find their long perspectives in the stars and
> galaxies; I prefer the earthbound scale of the biological . . . In
> the rich black crumbly mulch I saw two black ants, a springtail,
> and a dark red worm-like creature with a score of pale brown

legs. These were the rumbling giants of this lower world, for not far below the threshold of visibility was the seething world of the roundworms – the scavengers and the predators who fed on them, and even these were giants relative to the inhabitants of the microscopic realm, the parasitic fungi and the bacteria – perhaps ten million of them in this handful of soil . . . What I thought might calm me was the reminder that, for all our concerns, we were still part of this natural dependency – for the animals that we ate grazed the plants which, like our vegetables and fruits, were nourished by the soil formed by these organisms. But even as I squatted to enrich the forest floor, I could not believe in the primary significance of these grand cycles. Just beyond the oxygen-exhaling trees stood my poison-exuding vehicle, inside which was my gun, and thirty-five miles down teeming roads was the enormous city where a madman was waiting, and my threatened loved one. What, in this description, was necessary to the carbon cycle, or the fixing of nitrogen? We were no longer in the great chain. It was our own complexity that had expelled us from the Garden. We were in a mess of our own unmaking. I stood and buckled my belt and then with the diligence of a household cat, kicked the soil back into my trench.[14]

I began by saying that George Eliot's interest in natural history led her to be interested in the inexorable movements of natural laws, and thus in probable and typical human conditions and actions. In *Middlemarch* her narrative voice remarks on 'that element of tragedy which lies in the very fact of frequency' and says that if we were conscious of it, 'perhaps our frames could hardly bear much of it. If we had a keen vision and feeling of all ordinary human life, it would be like hearing the grass grown, and the squirrel's heart beat, and we should die of that roar which lies on the other side of silence'. [15] By the time she wrote *Daniel Deronda*, her last novel, which Barbara Hardy says is in some ways a 'sensation novel' akin to the melodramas of Wilkie Collins, she is more interested than she was in the workings of violent accident and blind chance. As I said, it seems significant that Gwendolen is discovered playing games of hazard. In the same way, the twentieth-century Darwinian novelists seem to have shifted their interest from the laws of development to the operations of hazard. McEwan's plots are close to those of modern genre fictions, thrillers and artificially plotted mysteries. The gun which goes off in the restaurant kills a stranger, and McEwan gives this stranger enough of a life and a family, and a character, for his readers to imagine the effects of this purely hazardous event on lives which might have appeared to have had quite other forms. Something analogous is going on in Peter Carey's *Oscar and Lucinda*, where the protagonists conduct their lives and deaths, according to card-games, and bets – this in the context of Oscar's being the son of a naturalist based on Philip Gosse who believed that there was a particular providence in the creation of all creatures (and all fossils). I remember, myself, being so angry with D.H. Lawrence for declaring in *Women in Love* that there were no accidents, that every man made his own fate, that I constructed a novel with at least six main characters so that I could imagine a real, unpredicted, random accident at the end of the second volume, that my readers would experience *as accident*. They did and do – they still write to reproach me as though I was indeed God and had killed my character, Stephanie, wilfully to hurt them, the readers. (Which I suppose, in some sense, I had.) John Fowles's narrator, in *The French Lieutenant's Woman*, claims that the Victorian third-person narrator is playing God, omniscient and all-powerful, and tries to claim the space of what he explicitly calls the 'aleatory' novel.

> The novelist is still a god, since he creates (and not even the most aleatory avant-garde novel has managed to extirpate its author completely); what has changed is that we are no longer the gods of the Victorian image, omniscient and decreeing; but in the new theological image, with freedom our first principle, not authority.[16]

I don't myself believe that George Eliot's narrative voice is that of an omniscient God, still less of a decreeing one – I think she saw it as much nearer to the common human voice of the Chorus in Greek Tragedy. What is interesting is that the idea of 'freedom' (in Fowles) and the introduction of the value, against belief, of particular individuals (McEwan, Swift, Barnes) seems to go with contrived and *overtly plotted* narration which, as Keats said 'has designs on the reader'. This is partly because nineteenth-century high realism is only one form of storytelling, with one set of assumptions about how we think of ourselves. The interesting ones are not necessarily those foregrounded by Fowles. A book which has recently fascinated me, both as a reader, as a writer, and as a human being, is Ian Hacking's extraordinary study of the new forms of determinism introduced into human thought by the study of chance, of statistical probability, of the idea of the 'normal', the average, the probable human being. Hacking's book begins

> The most decisive conceptual event of twentieth-century physics has been the discovery that the world is not deterministic. Causality, long the bastion of metaphysics, was toppled, or at least tilted: the past does not determine exactly what happens next. This event was preceded by a more gradual transformation. During the nineteenth century it became possible to see that the world might be regular and yet not subject to universal laws of nature. A space was cleared for chance.[17]

Hacking's book suddenly made it clear to me what was going on in Penelope Fitzgerald's *The Gate of Angels*,[18] a delightful comedy which, like all her novels, tugs at the consciousness of her readers with the sense that there is more here, more significance, than the sheer pleasure of the elegant prose and the satisfactory storytelling. Like many of the Darwinian novels I have discussed, it contains both the crisis of faith and the salvation of romantic love. It is set in Cambridge in 1907, and its hero, Fred Fairly, is a physicist. He goes to tell his clergyman father that he has lost his faith, reflecting that this crisis will not be like 'the giant battles from what seemed like heroic days' when in the 1850s two of his uncles quarrelled over Strauss's *Leben Jesu* 'and struck each other and one of them had caught his head on the edge of the fender and broken his skull. The other one, Uncle Philip, had been known for the rest of his life, though never in the family, as Slayer Fairly.' Fred imagines himself saying to his father 'the only evidence we can get is from our senses and from the senses of other people who have gone before us' but in fact his father cuts him short, telling him that he knew when Fred decided to study Natural Sciences 'you would sooner or later come to the conclusion that you had no further use for the soul. All I ask is that you shouldn't talk to me about it.' Fred is studying physics, in the glorious days of Rutherford's experiments at the Cavendish, under a maverick professor, Flowerdew, who also believes in the evidence of his senses, and dismisses the new atomic physics in a glorious diatribe.

'Let me tell you what is going to happen, over the centuries, to atomic research . . . The physicists will begin by constructing models of the atom, in fact there are some very nice ones in the Cavendish at the moment. Then they'll find that the models won't do, because they would only work if atoms really existed, so they'll replace them by mathematical terms which can be stretched to fit. As a result, they'll find that since they're dealing with what they can't observe they can't measure it, and so we shall hear that all that can be said is that the position is probably this and the energy is probably that. The energy will be beyond their comprehension, so they'll be driven to the theory that it comes and goes more or less at random. Now their hypotheses will be at the beginning of collapse and they will have to pull out more and more bright notions to paper over the cracks and to cram into unsightly corners. There will be elementary particles which are too strange to have anything but curious names, and anti-matter which ought to be there, but isn't. By the end of the century they will have to admit that the laws they are supposed to have discovered seem to act in a profoundly disorderly way. What is a disorderly law, Fairly?'

'It sounds like chaos,' said Fred.

'The chaos will be in their minds only. It too, will not be observable.'

'What do you think is to be done?'

'Admit the wrong direction and go back to what can be known by the senses.' . . . Herbert Flowerdew had been offered a temporary Professorship in Observable Experimental Physics.

Fred finds himself, at a university society called the Disobligers, where members are required to argue against their own convictions, having to make a speech in defence of the immortal soul, and he puts up a good case for the independence of the mind from the body. Here, reduced to lovely rhetoric, is the fallacious infinity in the finite,

> 'Fellow-members and Disobligers I reject reason. I stand here this evening as a believer. I believe in gravitation without weight, life without organic matter, thought without nervous tissue, voices and apparitions without known cause, water turned into wine, stones rolled back without motive power, and souls without bodies. More than that, I believe that the grass is green because green is restful to the human eye, that the sky is blue to give us an idea of the infinite, and that blood is red so that murder will be more easily detected and criminals will be brought to justice. Yes, and I believe that I shall live forever, but I shall live without reason.'

Reason and poetry – the opposition also of *Enduring Love*. The romantic plot of *The Gate of Angels* is constructed by outrageous coincidence and extravagant chance. Fred falls in love with Daisy, who is working-class and a nurse, which is a mundane form of 'angel'. Daisy is in Cambridge because she tried to restore the interest in life of a suicidal young man (who had attempted to drown himself in the Thames), by persuading a newspaper editor to report his death. The editor is not interested, because he sees the young man as a statistic. Much of the early excitement about probability was provided by the statistics of the regularity of the annual number of suicides in Paris, which interested both Durkheim and Richard Buckle. Daisy attempts to turn her young patient from a statistic into a tragic individual. What happens is that she loses her job, and is driven to accept an invitation from the editor to spend a weekend as a married woman in Cambridge. She and Fred are accidentally and simultaneously knocked off their bicycles by a horse and cart, and wake up naked next to each other, since they are assumed to be married. (Daisy is wearing a wedding ring for her immoral weekend.) Misunderstandings follow. Fred's college – St Angelicus – has a rule that no women may ever enter for any reason. It also has a gate which is

never opened. Daisy, after a disastrous separation and misunder-
standing, finds the gate open and steps in just in time to save the life
of the blind Master of the College, who suffers a syncope. This delays
her, the last sentence tells us, enough to meet Fred Fairly walking
slowly back to St Angelicus. And to undo the misunderstandings, we
are to suppose.

Are atoms, in their unpredictability and invisibility and
randomness a new form of angel? Fitzgerald is playing lightly with the
random and the haphazard, in the form of her novel and in life, in
defence of the concept of chance, which gives an importance to the
individual life, the particular feeling. No one is only a statistic, though
everyone is a statistic. Hacking says, in his first chapter that 'parallel
to the taming of chance of which I speak there arose a self-conscious
conception of pure irregularity, of something wilder than the kinds of
chance that had been excluded by the Age of Reason. It harked back,
in part, to something ancient or vestigial. It also looked into the
future, to new, and often darker, visions of the person . . . Its most
passionate spokesman was Nietzsche. Its most subtle and many-
layered expression was Mallarmé's poem "Un coup de dés".' In his
section on Nietzsche, Hacking quotes Fitzgerald's dead poet, Novalis,
on the miraculous

> The poet Novalis had written in 1797 that chance manifests
> the miraculous. The individual is 'individualized by one single
> chance event alone, his birth'. In Zarathustra this idea blazed
> forth in a famous blessing:
> 'To stand over every single thing as its own round roof, its
> azure bell . . . Over all things stand the heaven accident, the
> heaven innocence, the heaven chance, the heaven
> prankishness.
> '"By chance" – that is the most ancient nobility of the
> world, and this I restored to all things: I delivered them from
> their bondage under purpose.'

Heaven is turned into a 'dance floor for divine accidents', a 'divine
table for divine dice and divine dice players'. How then did rationality
arrive in the world? 'Irrationally as might be expected: by a chance
accident.'[19]

Fitzgerald describes a comic miracle, creates a comic, chancy form, which reflects a Romantic and post-romantic, post-realist, idea of the human individual which is still making new novels.

· 4 ·

True Stories and the Facts in Fiction

'Better and better, man. Would now St Paul would come along that way, and to my breezelessness bring his breeze! O Nature, and O soul of man! how far beyond all utterance are your linked analogies! not the smallest atom stirs or lives on matter, but has its cunning duplicate in mind.' Herman Melville, *Moby Dick*, Chapter LXIX, 'The Sphinx'.

'He fashions each natural object to a theologic notion; a horse signifies carnal understanding; a tree, perception; the moon, faith; a cat means this; an ostrich that; an artichoke this other; – and poorly tethers every symbol to a several ecclesiastic sense. The slippery Proteus is not so easily caught. In Nature, each individual symbol plays innumerable parts, as each particle of matter circulates in turn through every system. The central identity enables any one symbol to express successively all the qualities and shades of real being. In the transmission of the heavenly waters, every hose fits every hydrant. Nature avenges herself speedily on the hard pedantry that would chain her waves.' R.W. Emerson 'Swedenborg; or the Mystic' from *Representative Men*.

'I must buy that. It would give me new metaphors.' A poet, my friend, on the telephone, after my enthusiastic recommendation of E.O. Wilson's *Insect Societies*.

I

This essay is about the relations of precise scholarship and fiction – largely historical fiction. The example I have used is the writing of my two linked historical novellas, *Morpho Eugenia* and *The Conjugial Angel*, published together as *Angels and Insects*. The first version of the essay was written shortly after I finished writing the stories, and reflects the moment to moment preoccupations with problems of accuracy and invention of the writing.

Both stories arise directly from my teaching in the English Department of University College London. It is customary for writer-academics to claim a kind of schizoid personality, and state that their research, or philosophical thinking, has nothing to do with their work as makers of fiction. I don't know whether this is from fear of being thought to be amateurs in one or the other of their professions, or from fear, particularly in Britain, that the rigorous forms of the life of the intellect might be felt to inhibit their 'creativity'. I have myself always felt that reading and writing and teaching were all part of some whole that it was dangerous to disintegrate. *The Conjugial Angel* sprang directly from a lecture I used to give on the presence of Arthur Henry Hallam in Tennyson's *In Memoriam*. *Morpho Eugenia* is related to the reading of Darwin in connection with George Eliot's novels and essays, and also to modern Darwinian ideas and fictions. The same ideas could have turned into academic papers on 'Swedenborg, Spiritualism, the energetic principle of love for the beautiful, The Human Form Divine and other uses of the human body in *In Memoriam*'. Or 'Arthur Hallam, Alfred Tennyson, Emily Tennyson and Emily Tennyson: Male Friendship and Victorian Women'. Or 'The Life after Death in the Victorian Imagination' or 'Sexual Selection and Insect Societies in Victorian Thought'. Or 'The Earthly Paradise: Adam, Linnaeus, Wallace, Bates, the English Hedgerow and the Amazon Jungle'.

Why did these particular ideas form themselves into fictions?

This question brings up the question of why the past is the subject of so much modern fiction. When I began writing novels, we were being lectured by C.P. Snow and Kingsley Amis about how good fiction *ought to* describe the serious social concerns of contemporary society. It seemed perfectly adequate to dismiss historical fiction as 'escapism', and defences were unconvincing, apart from Lukàcs's powerful account of the European Walter Scott. We were later exhorted by Malcolm Bradbury and the *Guardian* to find new forms, now-this-minute, to describe the collapse of communism and Thatcher's Britain. The fall of the Berlin Wall, Bradbury rightly says, has changed our world. There should be new fictive forms, he also says, experimental forms, based perhaps on new means of information, television, satellite surveillance, to take on these rapid changes.

And yet there is a large body of serious and ambitious fiction set in the past, not for the pleasures of escapism or bodice-ripping, but for complex aesthetic and intellectual reasons. Some of it is sober and some of it is fantastic, some of it is knowing and postmodernist, some of it is feminist or post-colonial rewritings of official history, some of it is past prehistory, some of it is very recent. The writers include William Golding, Anthony Burgess, Julian Barnes, Angela Carter, Graham Swift, J.M. Coetzee, Italo Calvino, Christoph Ransmayr, Jeanette Winterson, Barry Unsworth, Michèle Roberts, Marina Warner, Jane Rogers, Caryl Phillips, Timothy Mo, Peter Ackroyd, Peter Carey, Elaine Feinstein, Penelope Fitzgerald and Toni Morrison – and many more.

There are all sorts of possible reasons for this. One, I think, which certainly affects me, is the vanishing of the past from the curriculum of much modern education in schools and increasingly in colleges and universities. 'A' Level courses are increasingly preoccupied with contemporary texts to which students can hypothetically 'relate'. And yet my sense of my own identity is bound up with the past, with what I read and with the way my ancestors, genetic and literary, read, in the worlds in which they lived. A preoccupation with ancestors has always been part of human make-up, and still, I think comes naturally. Freud wrote in 1933

Science is very young – a human activity which developed late. Let us bear in mind, to select only a few dates, that only some 300 years have passed since Kepler discovered the laws of planetary movement, that the life of Newton, who analysed light into the colours of the spectrum and laid down the theory of gravitation, ended in 1727 – that is to say, little more than

200 years ago – and that Lavoisier discovered oxygen shortly before the French revolution. The life of an individual is very short in comparison with the duration of human evolution; I may be a very old man today, but nevertheless I was already alive when Darwin published his book on the origin of species. And if you go further back, to the beginnings of exact science among the Greeks, to Archimedes, to Aristarchus of Samos, (about 250 BC) who was the forerunner of Copernicus, or even to the first beginnings of astronomy among the Babylonians, you will only have covered a small fraction of the length of time which anthropologists require for the evolution of man from an ape-like ancestral form, and which certainly comprises more than a hundred thousand years.[1]

The older I get, the more I habitually think of my own life as a relatively short episode in a long story of which it is a part. Darwin and Freud – and Tennyson, and even Swedenborg – do seem to me more central and urgent in this story than much of what is on television (in which I am also interested) or even the day to day movements in Kuwait or Sarajevo. It is always said of Browning's various resurrected pasts in his dramatic monologues that they are about Browning and the nineteenth century, and of course this is true – but it is not always added that they are also truly about the time when the New Testament was written, or about Renaissance Christianity and Art, though they are, and are illuminating about those matters. It is not either – or. At its best it is both – and. I do believe that if I read *enough*, and carefully enough, I shall have some sense of what words meant in the past, and how they related to other words in the past, and be able to use them in a modern text so that they do not lose their relations to other words in the interconnected web of their own vocabulary. At a time when certain kinds of criticism and ideological activity are happy to dispense with close attention to the history of words and their uses, it seems somehow important to be able to make coherent texts using words as they were used, together.[2] Writing serious historical fiction today seems to me to have something in common with the difficult modern enterprise of Borges's Pierre Menard, rewriting the Quixote, in the 'same' words, now.

*

This brings me to language. The journalist Chris Peachment interviewed various novelists about ten years ago about why they were
writing historical novels, expecting some answer about paradigms of
contemporary reality, and got the same answer from all of them. They
wanted to write in a more elaborate, more complex way, in longer
sentences, and with more figurative language. (I think the novelists
interviewed were Golding, Ackroyd, Fowles and Swift but am not sure
about this.) This surprised Chris Peachment but interested me. I
associated this answer with a story of John Cheever,[3] 'MENE, MENE,
TEKEL,UPHARSIN', in which a man finds that the graffiti in an imposing
marble-partitioned gentlemen's lavatory are long literary-aesthetic
paragraphs, and with Anthony Burgess's *1985* where the skinheads are
secretly learning Latin in garages, because it is forbidden. Cheever's
narrator is baffled by forms resembling (or perhaps they are) Poe, Pater
and Wilde, and compares the archaic texts to the paperback books of
'graphic descriptions of sexual commerce' in the 'noble waiting room'.
'What had happened, I supposed, was that, as pornography moved into
the public domain, those marble walls, those immemorial repositories
of such sport, had been forced, in self-defence, to take up the more
refined task of literature.' His final discovery in an airport men's room,
written on tile, is 'Bright Star! would I were stedfast as thou art – Not
in lone splendour hung aloft the night . . .' Rhetoric has become shady
and a secretive pleasure.

I do have a strong sense of what a good *modern* sentence is. I found
myself making this sense precise when I read V.S. Naipaul's novel, *The
Enigma of Arrival* (1987). A good modern sentence proceeds evenly,
loosely joined by commas, and its feel is hypothetical, approximate,
unstructured and always aiming at an impossible exactness which it
knows it will not achieve. Naipaul's book is about a very well-read
West Indian making sense of a local Wiltshire landscape and society
by constant revision of his preconceptions and constant formation and
reformation of new hypotheses. Consider, for example, the following
paragraphs from the first section, 'Jack's Garden', which begin with
precise enumerating description, and end with uncertainty about what
Jack saw in the same facts.

The elaborate garden, with all its time-eating chores, was flattened. What was left didn't need much attention. No bedding-out plants now; no forking over of the ground below the hawthorn tree; no delphiniums in the summer. The garden was flattened, all but two or three rose bushes and two or three apple trees which Jack had pruned in such a way that they bunched out at the top, from a thick straight trunk. And the ground was grassed over. The hedge, once tight at the top, mud-spattered and ragged at the bottom, a half or quarter barrier between garden and rutted farm-road, the hedge began to grow out into trees.

Now more than ever the cottages appeared to have neither front nor back, and to stand in a kind of waste ground. It matched the people and their attitude to the place. It matched the new way of farming, logic taken to extremes, the earth stripped finally of its sanctity – the way the pink thatched cottage on the public road, once pretty with its rose hedge, had been stripped of its atmosphere of home by the people who looked to it only for shelter.

But that might have been only my way of looking. I had known – for a short time – the straight stretch of the droveway open and unfenced. It had been fenced down the middle in my first year, and had remained fenced; but I carried that earlier picture. I had arrived at my feeling for the seasons by looking at Jack's garden, adding events on the river and the manor river bank to what I saw in his garden. But there were other ways of looking. Jack himself, giving the attention he gave to a meaningless hedge – a hedge that ran down the length of his garden and then abruptly stopped – saw something else, certainly.[4]

It is in a sense a paradigm of *scholarly* habits of mind, the search for impossible precision, and this, I think, can be said about other texts which strike me as quintessentially modern (always thinking on the Freudian timescale when the 1960s is a very short time ago). I think oddly of Doris Lessing's *The Golden Notebook* and more obviously of Michel Butor's *L'Emploi du Temps*, which is also about a foreigner making sense of an alien reality, in his case Manchester. Lessing's novel is about the breakdown of language and of fictive forms adequate to describe the sexual and political reality of the immediate present. All three texts are haunted by literary ancestors. Naipaul knows his Dickens and corrects his Dickensian London against 1950s reality. Butor, in his baffled text, alternates desperately precise passages of attempts to find geographical bearings with parodies of Proust's elaborate architectural cathedral metaphors. Lessing's novelist-heroine expresses exasperation that a text is no longer possible that can draw the whole world together as Tolstoi could.[5] Lessing demonstrates the fragmentary nature of the world her heroine lives in with a series of texts within texts, parodic and semi-parodic, a novel within a novel, parodies of women's magazine stories, sentimental film 'treatments' of novels, Stalinist narratives and theories, fragments of headlines, all made of different kinds of restricted vocabularies. The moments in the *prose* of *The Golden Notebook* that most excited me when I first read it were little self-correcting sequences of sentences about how to say things, how to get things right. I was haunted for years, without quite understanding why it was so important, by the following paragraph.[6]

> I've thought about that often since. I mean, about the word nice. Perhaps I mean good. Of course they mean nothing, when you start to think about them. A good man, one says; a good woman; a nice man, a nice woman. Only in talk of course, these are not words you'd use in a novel. I'd be careful not to use them.
>
> Yet, of that group, I will say simply, without further analysis, that George was a good person, and that Willi was not. That Maryrose and Jimmy and Ted and Johnnie the pianist were good people, and that Paul and Stanley Lett were not. And furthermore, I'd bet that ten people picked at random off the street to meet them, or invited to sit in that party under the eucalyptus trees that night would instantly agree with that classification – would, if I used the word *good*, simply like that, know what I meant.

The passage is about moral authority in the world and it is not insignificant that it is about a group of communists in Africa. But the phrase that haunted me as a writer was 'these are not words you'd use in a novel. I'd be careful not to use them.' Doris Lessing has made it possible for herself to use them by declaring her – or her heroine's – suspicion of them, her *care* as a writer to avoid them. Partly what moved me in the 1960s was the way it made me think about the vocabulary of a whole text as a *field*, a coherent field in which certain words worked and others didn't. But partly it was the excitement and freedom of the self-reflexive narrative transgression. 'I'd be careful not to –' she writes, and then does what she 'cannot' do. I think this is related at some distance to the way in which Menard's Quixote and Cervantes' Quixote are different fields, in which the words have different values. In a 'modern' text one may examine them in the questing way of Doris Lessing/Anna Wulf. Using words like 'good' in a modern text written with the loaded vocabulary, say, of the Victorian fairy tale, makes a different field again.

And the passages that troubled me, as well as exciting me, were the ones in which the novelist resisted her psychoanalyst's pleasure in her dreaming of ancient myths and paradigms and fairy tales. For these powerful metaphors and analogies, she felt, obscured and impeded her quest for the impossible accurate record of *now*. They were a form of aesthetic closure, agreeable, but not exactly useful. Anna tells the psychoanalyst she recognises her pleasure when she describes a dream of wolves, or ruined temples and blue seas.

> I know what the look means because I feel it myself – recognition. The pleasure of recognition, of a bit of rescue-work, so to speak, rescuing the formless into form. Another bit of chaos rescued and 'named'. Do you know how you smile when I 'name' something? It's as if you'd just saved someone from drowning . . . No sooner do you accomplish that than you say quickly – put it away, put the pain away where it can't hurt, turn it into a story or a history . . . I'm tired of the wolves and the castle and the forests and the priests. I can cope with them in any form they choose to present themselves. But I've told you, I want to walk off by myself, Anna Freeman.[7]

I connect this sense I have of fiction's preoccupation with impossible truthfulness with modern scholarship's increasing use of the techniques and attitudes of art. And indeed, artfulness. It is as though the two have changed places in a dance. Recent years have seen much discussion of the idea that history is fiction, and the understanding (not as new as it is sometimes said to be) that all narratives are partial and intrinsically biased. It has been pointed out that critics are writers, which of course they are and always have been – but emphasis on this fact is problematic in an academic establishment of literary studies where there still exists, in some sense, a body of primary texts that are the object of critical study. Barthes and others have put forward the idea that texts are constructed, in some sense 'written' by readers, which was an idea the writer in me used to find exciting before it became a commonplace. Writing a text does feel both the same as and different from reading one, and vice versa. But Barthes and others use it as a way of denying the authorship and authority of writers.

As writers of fiction become preoccupied with truthfulness and accuracy, writers of literary history and literary criticism seem to have taken on many of the rhetorical postures and attitudes of imaginative licence which once went with the artfulness of art. An example which springs to mind, because I reviewed it with a mixture of admiration[8] and irritation with its postures and style, is Mary Jacobus's *Romanticism, Writing and Sexual Difference*. Jacobus as writer claims her text with a series of erudite and not-so-erudite jokes and puns, often designed to diminish the writer she is studying, Wordsworth, who is characterised as 'the nutter of Nutting' and 'the spoiled brat of *The Prelude*'. She even manages to suggest that the paradigmatic narrative she is discussing requires the death of Wordsworth's mother, whether or not it happened in fact. What are we, as readers, to make of the tone of the following? What status as opinions or narrative or joke have these sentences?

> Wordsworth's mother really did die early. But Rousseau's *Emile* suggests that if she were not already dead, she would have to be killed off; that autobiography comes into being on the basis of a missing mother.[9]

The proposition itself is dubious, but it is the fictive 'killing off' that I find rhetorically interesting. By whom? When? In what real or invented world? I am also interested in the narrative posture of the writer who can say, discussing the narrative genre of *The Prelude*,

> Genre might be called the Frenchification of gender, and it
> was in France that (having left his French letters at home, as
> they say in England) Wordsworth discovered the literal
> implications of engendering.[10]

What relation do these anachronisms – nutter, French letter,
engendering of text – bear to the inventive anachronisms of Pierre
Menard, scholar and writer? What *use* are they to, what relationship do
they set up with, the reader of scholarly historical studies of
Wordsworth?

Mary Jacobus's project is to reread, and in a riddling sense to rewrite
The Prelude in the light of her own political preoccupations. Thus she
is able to tell her readers that

> the passions that blind the feminist reader to the text are one
> form of error that she might want to endorse. To paraphrase
> Rousseau on women readers, since 'The world is the book of
> women,' the feminist reader would be one who 'will read in
> men's [texts] better than they do' – while deliberately mis-
> reading in the blinding light of her own desire. Of course such
> a reading of *The Prelude* is itself didactic. Even error is
> deliberate, even blindness a form of knowledge . . .[11]

She is also able to construe Wordsworth's lines about 'Newton with his
prism and silent face/Voyaging o'er strange seas of thought, alone' as a
significant omission of the fact that Newtonian science had been used
in the development of navigation which had led to the slave trade,
which had been the occupation of the castaway, John Newton, who
had spent his solitude learning Euclid.[12] Her argument rests on the
coincidence of the names (it is true that Wordsworth had read John
Newton and quotes him – on geometry) – and a certainty of her own
right to judge Wordsworth's subject-matter. Slavery, right. Geometry,
wrong. These are the worthy political preoccupations of the 1980s.
This is Jacobus's text.

This is a kind of rewriting, or writing between the lines which fiction
does with more tact, less whimsy and infinitely more power. Caryl
Phillips's *Cambridge*, a modern nineteenth-century text, written by a

black man in the persona of a white woman visiting a slave plantation, rereads both the feminine novel of sensibility and the slave narratives. And Toni Morrison's great novel, *Beloved*, gives a voice, a new life, a life *now* to the silenced slaves of the slave narratives, and rewrites, or at least radically changes the reading of the great nineteenth-century American novels. Hawthorne, Melville, Poe, Twain and Stowe, oppose black and white, embody the fears and anxieties of white men, connect these with the colours of Heaven and Hell, however subtly, however variously. Morrison makes black skin into a rainbow of subtle colours and life, and makes white into the appalling *absence* that it is in Melville's chapter on 'The Whiteness of the Whale'. Poe's *Narrative of Arthur Gordon Pym* makes the abyss milky white – Morrison's imagery both endorses and shows up the human limitations of the uneasy understandings of Melville and Poe. Morrison's escaped slaves are fierce and real men and women. They transform the imagined world, permanently. Mary Jacobus complains that Wordsworth's poem leaves no openings for a female consciousness. Morrison simply *makes* new openings – black, female, both then and now.

Jacobus's rhetoric requires her to take a central and controlling and very visible position in her own text. It is a kind of deliberate vanity which it is instructive to compare with the extreme vanity of Norman Mailer in *Armies of the Night*, an account of the 1968 march on the Pentagon, divided into two parts, 'History as a Novel' and 'The Novel as History'. Mailer uses his own central consciousness as narrator, participant, and commentator to *exasperate* the reader with his egoism and partiality. He describes his own self-indulgent drunk rhetoric, the fact that he is attended on the protest march by a documentary film-crew concerned with his own self-advertisement, his overweening competitiveness with other writers present. He then asks the same reader to make sense of the later part of the story which the narrator did not see, the imprisonment of the Quaker pacifists, for which contradictory and obviously inadequate newspaper accounts have to be used. Even such a partial ordering consciousness – especially one so transparently partial – he is arguing, is more use than mere reporting. The result is technically interesting in terms of narrative, of figurative language, of the relations between objective and subjective recording or telling. Both Mailer and Jacobus exhibit their own partiality. But it is the fiction writer who believes that the idea of truth may, through all the obfuscation and rhetoric – his is supremely a text about rhetoric – have meaning.

It is perhaps no accident that my exemplary 'modern' texts are all written in the first person – a first person preoccupied with the desirability and impossibility of objectivity and truthfulness – and this is true even of Mailer's deliberate egocentric narration. I began as a writer with a deep mistrust of the first person – as a fictional narrative method, or as a voice for critical commentary. I think it is changes in the rhetoric of criticism that lead me to write commentary more and more overtly in an exploratory, and 'authorial' first person. I have only written one 'fictive' text in the first person,[13] which was the only one that consciously used these 'modern sentences' – *Sugar*, a family history cast as an autobiography. My instinct as a writer of fiction has been to explore and defend the unfashionable Victorian third-person narrator – who is not, as John Fowles claimed, playing at being God, but merely the writer, telling what can be told about the world of the fiction.

II
Imaginary Pasts

What follows is a brief, partial and exploratory account of the construction of my two historical fantasies, discussing the origins of the stories, the original ideas behind them, the 'research' both conventional and fictional, and the discoveries – for me – the writing led to. Informing both the stories and this account of the stories is the concern I have already tried to describe with the field of available language, with truthfulness or accuracy, and with appropriate rhetoric.

The Conjugial Angel, like 'Precipice-Encurled', a story I wrote about Browning in the 1880s, began with what might be called a marginalising footnote. In the case of 'Precipice-Encurled' it was in a book about Browning's hypothetical last love for Mrs Bronson in Venice. The author of the book recorded that Browning did not go to Ischia because a young house-guest of his prospective host had died after a fall from a cliff whilst sketching.[14] Absence of information starts the imagination working – I wondered about the dead young person whose life and death were contained in a footnote. (This is a professional extension of a normal reading process, in history or fiction, making a fuller, more vivid, more hypothetical narrative precisely around what we are *not* told.) In this case I decided to *invent* the faller – I did not even know whether it was a man or a woman – and to describe the fall, the sudden death, in a fully imagined third-person narrative, involving the reader as fiction does. Around this fictive window I arranged other pieces of narrative, in other styles – the 'hypothetical' style of the researcher, the borrowed quotations from Browning himself, about mountains, about accidents, about writing, narrative thefts from Henry James's story, 'The Private Life', itself a hypothetical and playful structure about the relations between the private and the public selves of Robert Browning.

The Conjugial Angel also started with a footnote – in this case a footnote to the *Collected Letters* of Arthur Henry Hallam, in which Fryn Tennyson Jesse, Emily Tennyson Jesse's granddaughter, tells the story of Emily's life after Arthur Hallam, to whom she was engaged when he died in 1833. The engagement had been forbidden until he was twenty-one, and they must have spent only a few weeks in each other's company. Emily mourned him until 1842, when she married Lieutenant Jesse, amid a cloud of contemptuous criticism – for instance from Elizabeth Barrett, who wrote

> Miss Tennyson is a very radically prosaic sister for the great poet, – does her best to take away the cadence and rhymes of the sentiment of life. What a disgrace to womanhood! The whole is a climax of *badness* – ! *to marry at all* – bad! – to keep the annuity, having married, – worse! to conglomerate and perpetuate the infidelity and indelicacy, by giving the sacred name to the offspring of the 'lubberly lieutenant' – worst of all!!! That last was a desperate grasp at a sentiment and missed.[15] [Emily's elder son was called Arthur Hallam Jesse.]

Fryn Tennyson Jesse tells the story of Emily Jesse's spiritualist experiences in the 1870s in Margate.

One spirit, I have always heard, told my grandmother that in the future life she would be reunited to Arthur Hallam, whereupon she turned to my grandfather and said indignantly: 'Richard, we may not always have got on together and our marriage may not have been a success, but I consider that an extremely unfair arrangement, and shall have nothing to do with it. We have been through bad times together in this world and I consider it only decent to share our good times, presuming we have them, in the next.'[16]

Emily Jesse, like Tennyson's brother Frederick, and another sister, Mary, did become members of Swedenborg's New Jerusalem Church. Swedenborg believed that angels were composed of a man and a woman conjoined, and that these androgynous angels were known as conjugial angels. My own interest in Swedenborg and in spiritualism came from working on Henry James, and the curious world of 'isms' – feminism, spiritualism, Swedenborgianism, Fourierism – which informs The Bostonians and led me back to Henry James the elder, who according to Emerson, 'wrote the Secret of Swedenborg and kept it'. Elizabeth Barrett Browning, like many of her contemporaries, took these things with passionate seriousness, and Balzac, so often thought of as the arch materialist and realist, cannot be understood without understanding his Swedenborgian interests – his short novel, Séraphita, is an account of the marriage of a conjugial angel to itself. Alex Owen's excellent book, The Darkened Room,[17] is a gripping feminist account of nineteenth-century mediumship as one of the few professions open to women, and one which relied heavily on what were traditionally thought of as 'feminine' qualities of passivity, receptiveness, lack of 'reason'.

The original impulse for The Conjugial Angel was in this sense revisionist and feminist. It would tell the untold story of Emily, as compared to the often-told story of Arthur and Alfred in which Emily is a minor actress. I would write the seance in which the angel appeared and was rejected.

One of my données was Emily Tennyson's exclusion. She was excluded from Hallam Tennyson's Life of his father after Hallam's death, though he recorded the scene where she first came downstairs after a year of secluded mourning 'with a white flower in her hair as he liked to see her'. She was almost excluded from *In Memoriam*, apart from Tennyson's reference to Hallam's possible marriage and his own possible nephews and nieces.

> I see thee sitting crowned with good,
> A central warmth diffusing bliss
> In glance and smile, and clasp and kiss,
> On all the branches of thy blood;
>
> Thy blood, my friend, and partly mine;
> For now the day was drawing on,
> When thou shouldst link thy life with one
> Of mine own house and boys of thine
>
> Had babbled 'Uncle' on my knee;
> But that remorseless iron hour
> Made cypress of her orange flower,
> Despair of Hope, and earth of thee.[18]
> (*In Memoriam A.H.H.* LXXXIV)

Although *In Memoriam* ends with the celebration of a marriage, the marriage is that of another sister, Cecilia, to another Apostle, Edmund Lushington. Tennyson talks steadily of himself as the widow in the poem. I thought about this, and tried to imagine what Emily Tennyson may have thought and felt.

It was in this context that I came up against the problem I initially thought this paper was 'about' – how far can one change 'truth' in fiction. I found myself troubled about Emily Tennyson herself – she had a dry wit, in what letters of hers I had read, and a rhapsodic note I was less happy with. If I had been writing biography or literary history I should have ransacked the papers at the Tennyson centre in Lincoln – whereas as a writer of fiction, I felt a strong inclination to *stop* with the information I had, from Hallam's letters, Fryn Tennyson Jesse, and various writings of Sir Charles Tennyson. I had the facts my imagination wanted to fantasise about, and I wanted space for the kind of female consciousness I needed, to which perhaps Emily Tennyson did not quite fit. Partly to get round this, I decided to invent two mediums – Lilias Papagay and Sophy Sheekhy – named for the female angels often described as having been in Paradise before Adam, Lilith and Sophia or the Shekhinah, who according to some theologies created matter. Mrs Papagay represents one reason for involvement in spiritualism – narrative curiosity. She is interested in people, their stories and secrets, she *will* imagine, she is a version of Sludge-as-Browning, the medium as artist or historian. Sophy actually *sees* things, images, finally both Hallam and the halfangel. She likes poems and is impatient of novels. I also invented a Swedenborgian *flamen* called Mr Hawke, and a grieving mother of five dead infant daughters, Mrs Hearnshaw. Mrs Papagay and Sophy, like Joshua, the cliff-faller in *Precipice-Encurled*, were my 'window' for pure fictive activity, and made it less necessary to *make up* Emily Jesse, so to speak. (In the sense in which Virginia Woolf speaks lovingly in her notebooks of mornings spent 'making up' the characters of *The Waves* or *The Years*.)

But I was also interested in both Tennyson and Hallam. (Indeed I only came to be interested in Emily because *In Memoriam* is a very great poem, and I did not want to forget that.) My interest in Hallam started with an observation of Marshall McLuhan's in a brilliant essay of 1951, 'Tennyson and Picturesque Poetry' in which he discussed Hallam's review in 1831 of Tennyson's poems.[19] Hallam praised Tennyson for being, in Keats's terms, a 'Poet of Sensation rather than Thought'. McLuhan connects Hallam's praise of sensuous images to modernist imagism, and sees Tennyson's landscape poems as precursors of symbolist landscape (*The Waste Land*).

> Whereas in external landscape diverse things lie side by side, so in psychological landscape the juxtaposition of various things and experiences becomes a precise musical means of orchestrating that which could never be rendered by systematic discourse. Landscape is the means of presenting, without the copula of logical enunciation, experiences which are united in existence but not in conceptual thought. Syntax becomes music, as in Tennyson's 'Mariana'.

McLuhan thought Hallam and Tennyson did not take the final step into cubist 'landscape of the mind' which 'puts the spectator always in the centre of the picture, whereas in picturesque art the spectator is always outside'. But when I read this essay I was already influenced by the morals of the fictions of Iris Murdoch and Doris Lessing who are both afraid of the mind losing external reality in an arrangement of images and analogies. Both Lessing and Murdoch are concerned in their fiction, and in their other writings, to detect the dangerous distorting power of 'fantasy'. I liked Hallam and Tennyson because their sensuousness was a guarantee of something resistant 'out there' as opposed to *paysage intérieur*.

So I read all Hallam's essays, and his translations of Dante, and much later, his letters (first published in 1981) and found that he had a cosmic myth of a Creator so much in need of Love that he created His Son in order to experience 'direct, immediate, absorbing affection for one object, on the ground of similarity perceived, and with a view to more complete union',[20] and that he created His Son as the object of his love, and the Universe as it is, full of sin and sorrow, as the necessary solution of the difficulty of making an object of Love finite, less perfect, not identical to the Lover, though still divine. Both Hallam's aesthetic and his theology are erotic, and material.

Thomas Mann once said that the *directed* reading for a piece of fiction was one of the great pleasures of his work. (He was talking about *Dr Faustus*). Once I had a framework and characters I simply immersed myself – over a period of years – in a disparate set of texts. Biographical texts about Hallams, Tennysons and Swedenborg. Swedenborg's writings. Angels in dictionaries of angels, and the Book of Revelation. Victorian theories of the afterlife. *In Memoriam*, again and again. It is a process like trawling, or knitting, and recurring themes and patterns began to make themselves. Birds, for instance. Emily Tennyson kept a pet raven. Swedenborg said that the thoughts of angels were perceived in the world of spirits in material form as birds. He also said that ravens and owls were symbols of evils and falses [sic] because they were birds of night (Emerson was right to detect something pedestrian in his symbolism). *In Memoriam* is haunted by birds – larks, linnets, doves, nightingales, rooks,

> birds the charming serpent draws
> To drop head-foremost in the jaws
> Of vacant darkness and to cease. (XXXIV)

Tennyson's poem 'Recollections of the Arabian Nights' uses the nightingale as a symbol of deathlessness, like Keats's Ode. This bird sings something which is

> Not he: but something which possessed
> The darkness of the world, delight,
> Life, anguish, death, immortal love,
> Ceasing not, mingled, unrepressed,
> Apart from place, withholding time

and is surely related to the later bird of *In Memoriam*, LXXXVIII

> Wild bird, whose warble, liquid sweet,
> Rings Eden through the budded quicks,
> O tell me where the senses mix,
> O tell me where the passions meet,
>
> Whence radiate: fierce extremes employ
> Thy spirits in the darkening leaf,
> And in the midmost heart of grief
> Thy passion clasps a secret joy:

Emily Tennyson, on the other hand, wrote a most prosaic, *outsider's* account of a real nightingale in Lincolnshire to Hallam's sister, after his death.[21] Michael Wheeler has pointed out that Rossetti, in his illustrations, connected Poe's raven in *Nevermore* with the vision of the conjoined Lovers in the heaven of the Blessed Damosel, since both were illustrated by him with one left-behind-mourner on earth and conjugial angels in heaven.[22] There is a pleasure to be found in making up real fictive birds and connecting them with images already active in the field of the language the fiction draws on.

I found, as I went on reading, that I was feeling out, or understanding, the Victorian fear that we *are* our bodies, and that, after death, all that occurs is natural mouldering. *In Memoriam* is permeated by Tennyson's desire to *touch* Hallam, Hallam's hands, particularly, and speculation about the decay of the body, tossed with tangle and with shells, netted by the roots of the yew in earth, eaten by worms.

I wage not any feud with Death
For changes wrought on form and face;
No lower life that earth's embrace
May breed with him, can fright my faith. (LXXXII)

Spiritualism offers precisely the reassurance of the bodily identity of the departed – they can indeed *touch* and make themselves apparent to the senses. Intelligent thinkers like James John Garth Wilkinson defended Swedenborg's religious beliefs, and Swedenborg's account of his own journeys in the worlds of angels, devils and spirits, as a proper faith for a *materialist* age, and were comforted by the conjunction of metallurgist and visionary in Swedenborg himself. Tennyson was able, 'thro' repeating my own name two or three times to myself silently' to put himself into a state of trance, where

> out of the intensity of the consciousness of individuality, the individuality itself seemed to dissolve and fade away into boundless being, and this not a confused state, but the clearest of the clearest, the surest of the surest, the weirdest of the weirdest, utterly beyond words, where death was an almost laughable impossibility, the loss of personality (if so it were) seeming no extinction but the only true life.[23]

'This might', he said, 'be the state which St Paul describes, 'Whether in the body I cannot tell, or whether out of the body I cannot tell.'' [24]

St Paul's story of the man who was caught up into the third heaven 'whether in the body, I cannot tell; whether out of the body, I cannot tell,' which I only knew in terms of Tennyson's trances turned out to be a recurring image. Swedenborg used it to preface his own visits to Heaven and Hell, Hallam read Dante who uses the same passage to prefigure his own bodily journey to Heaven at the beginning of the *Paradiso*. Tennyson's assertion 'I loved thee Spirit, and love, nor can/The soul of Shakespeare love thee more' reads differently in terms of this preoccupation with the afterlife of the body. Discoveries keep on happening. It was only on checking Keats's letter in which he wrote 'Oh for a life of Sensations rather than Thoughts!' that I found that he spoke in the next sentence of enjoying the same bodily pleasures in the afterlife as here on earth.[25]

The Conjugial Angel is a ghost story and a love story. As a ghost story it is concerned with live and dead bodies; as a love story it is concerned, among other things, with male and female bodies. One of my early germs of story was a letter of Hallam to Emily in which he talks about the *Theodicaea Novissima*. He says

> I was half inclined to be sorry that you looked into that Theodicaea of mine. It must have perplexed rather than cleared your sight of these high matters. I do not think women ought to trouble themselves much with theology: we, who are more liable to the subtle objections of the Understanding, have more need to handle the weapons that lay them prostrate. But where there is greater innocence, there are larger materials for a single-hearted faith. It is by the heart, not by the head, that we must all be convinced of the two great fundamental truths, the reality of Love and the reality of Evil. Do not, my beloved Emily, let any cloudy mistrusts and perplexities bewilder your perception of these, and of the great corresponding Fact, I mean the Redemption, which makes them objects of delight instead of horror. Be not deceived: we are not called to effect a reconciliation between the purity of God and our own evil: that is done freely for us . . . All our unhappiness comes from want of trust and reliance on the insatiable love of God.[26]

What interests me in this, apart from the usual patronising tone towards women, is the vocabulary of heart and head, feeling and thought. We have seen that Hallam set feeling before thought in poetry, and here he makes the completely usual conventional distinction between men and women as creatures of thought and feeling respectively. Tennyson too, in *In Memoriam*, uses the same convention. Lyrics XXXI to XXXIII deal with the Lazarus story. XXXI asks whether the resurrected man had desired to hear his sister weeping, and where he had been, which 'remaineth unrevealed'. XXXII is about the deep love of Mary Magdalene for both 'the living brother's face' and for Christ, 'the Life indeed'. XXXIII admonishes an undefined 'thou'

Whose faith has centre everywhere
Nor cares to fix itself to form,

Leave thou thy sister when she prays,
Her local Heaven, her happy views;
Nor thou with shadowed hint confuse
A life that leads melodious days.
Her faith through form is pure as thine,
Her hands are quicker unto good:
O sacred be the flesh and blood
To which she links a truth divine!

This is an application of 'O for a Life of Sensations rather than Thoughts' to theology. The woman is happier because her response to the Christian faith is through form, to flesh and blood – and I could spend a whole paper teasing out the complexities of placing these sentiments just here in this poem, next to Lazarus, the riddling exemplar of bodily survival of death. *Whose* flesh and blood? *Whose* sister? Here the Incarnation and the death of the body appear differently to male and female. But I want at this point only to emphasise the connection of woman with flesh and matter and of man with mind. This is an example of thinking by false analogies – impregnation of females by male semen, impregnation of inert Matter by the divine Nous, which I think all feminists ought to deconstruct. Instead of which many of them have aligned themselves with earth religions of the Mother, as though both men and women were not both body and spirit or mind, related in complicated ways. This is an analogy which has always troubled me since I first met it in seventeenth-century neoplatonism, and which tends to turn up in my writings when I am not looking, as though it was what I was really looking for all along. Once I saw that it was at work – *really and naturally* at work – in *The Conjugial Angel* all sorts of other discoveries began to connect to it, like filings attracted to a magnet. For instance, that the literary society formed by the Tennyson sisters and some women friends to discuss the sensuous poems of Keats, Shelley and Tennyson was called The Husks (how sad) and that their highest term of praise was 'deadly'. Or for instance that Swedenborg's female angels corresponded to 'good, will and affection' in Heaven, whilst the males were 'Truth, understanding and thought' but that after marriage the qualities were all part of the male, to whom the female was subordinated, as the Church was to Christ. And I found a wonderful piece of theology in Swedenborg for my final fictional seance.

Swedenborg believed that the whole Universe was one Divine Human, containing both male and female conjoined, and that heaven and hell were situated within this Divine Human, attached to the appropriate corresponding organs. He also claimed to have revealed, himself, to angels and to inhabitants of other planets, that the Divine Human had been incarnate in a finite human body, at one point in space and time, on earth, in Christ. Swedenborg taught that the incarnate Lord had *both* a mortal human form from his mother, and an eternal human form from the fact of his Divine Self, his Father. On earth he successively *put off* the Human assumed from the Mother, and put on the Human from the Divine in himself. He had two states on earth, one called the state of humiliation or exinanition, the other the state of glorification or union with the Divine, which is called the Father. He was in a state of humiliation or exinanition so far as, and when, He was in the human from the mother, and in a state of glorification so far as, and when, He was in the Human from the Father. His Crucifixion was a necessary shedding of the corrupt humanity He had from the mother, in order to experience glorification and union with the Father.[27]

Here the same analogies between women and matter (dead or deathly matter in this case) and men as mind are at work as are at work, *mutatis mutandis*, in Hallam's mixture of Keatsian sensuality and neo-platonic theology. I don't have time to go into the relations between mind and matter in *In Memoriam* though the story does. Nor do I have time to tell the story. But I will say briefly how the discoveries of the metaphors at work changed the writing.

Firstly it meant that the whole story became very *fleshly*, both about the living, real and imaginary, and about the dead. When Sophy Sheekhy does see the dead Hallam the important thing about him – though he speaks – is that he is a *dead body*, a dead weight, and clay-like – I took some images from the terrible dead man in Keats's sensuous and ghostly masterpiece, *Isabella*. The Hallam Sophy encounters knows that poems are the sensuous afterlife of men.

In the second place, it led towards the way to write the fact, (according to Fryn Tennyson Jesse) that the Jesses' seances were given up because of obscene messages. I wrote a series of obscene theological stanzas in the metre of *In Memoriam* incorporating something I found in Jung's *Alchemical Studies* about Sophia and the calling of chaos into matter,[28] and a reference to the stinking corpse of Fair Rosamond actually made by Hallam in his review of Tennyson – more specifically of the 'Dreams of the Arabian Nights" – where he quotes the 'monkish tag' – *non redolet sed olet, quae redolere solet.* 'Bees may be redolent *of* honey; spring may be "redolent *of* youth and love;" but the absolute use of the word has, we fear, neither in Latin nor English any better authority than the monastic epitaph on Fair Rosamond; "*Hic jacet in tomba Rosa Mundi, non Rosa Munda, non redolet, sed olet, quae redolere solet.*" '[29]

I wrote

. . .The Holy Ghost trawls in the Void
With fleshly Sophy on His Hook
The Sons of God crowd round to look
At plumpy limbs to be enjoyed

The Greater Man casts out the line
With dangling Sophy as the lure
Who howls around the Heavens' colure
To clasp the Human Form Divine. . . .

And is my Love become the Beast
That was, and is not, and yet is,
Who stretches scarlet holes to kiss
And clasps with claws the fleshly feast

Sweet Rosamund, adult'rous Rose
May lie inside her urn and stink
While Alfred's tears turn into ink
And drop into her *quelque-chose* . . .

And the third is a moment of fictive narrative I wrote in which Emily, the outsider, stands on the Somersby lawn, where Alfred and Arthur are trailing their hands, with their fingers not quite touching, and talking about divine love. Emily asks Arthur why *Hyle* is female and *Nous* is male, and he fobs her off in the tone of the *Theodicaea* letter. Later Alfred remembers the same scene – the hand he misses, an analogy with Michelangelo's God the Father and Adam (Hallam had 'the bar of Michelangelo' on his brow), 'the man I held as half-divine'. Emily has in her basket two texts Hallam sent her – *in fact* – *Emma* and *Undine*. He sent her Undine because he felt she resembled Undine in her wildness and naturalness. Undine was, I realised whilst writing this paper, a water-spirit without an immortal soul.

.I do not think I would have made many of the connections I made between Hallam's aesthetic, his theology, Emily's Swedenborgianism, the sociology of spiritualism, body and soul, by thinking in an orthodox scholarly way – or, for that matter in a deliberately *unorthodox* scholarly way, in feminist-deconstructionist critical puns. The direction of my research was wayward and precise simultaneously. And the combination of the pursuit of the excluded Emily and the attempt to understand the ideas and images of the two young men, did I think change my ideas about love and death in Victorian life and literature.

III

What I found – not, I think, imposed – in the writing of *The Conjugial Angel* was an anthropomorphic metaphor for the construction of the Universe, in its nineteenth-century form, though informed by many other versions. *Morpho Eugenia* is an entirely fictitious tale – intended as a kind of robust Gothic allegory, which initially I saw as a film, because one of its sources was the new visions of life afforded by cameras inside antheaps and termite hills. It had two germs. One was the observation that in *Middlemarch* Mr Farebrother the clergyman and collector of pinned dead insects was the old world order, and Lydgate, who wanted to examine living connective tissues, was the new. The other was Maeterlinck's anthropomorphic imagining of the Ant Queen after her nuptial flight. I read a great deal about insect life, for mixed reasons. I see insects as the Not-human, in some sense the Other, and I believe we ought to think about the not-human, in order to be fully human. Insects are the object of much anthropomorphising attention – we name their societies after our own, Queen, Soldier, Slave, Worker. I think we should be careful before we turn other creatures into images of ourselves, which explains why I was worried by my poet-friend's wish to find metaphors in E.O. Wilson's *Insect Societies*. Wilson's own extensions of his thought into human sociology have led to anxieties about political incorrectness, but he does have the ability to make us imagine the *antness* of his ants – at least as construed by this particular scientist. Maeterlinck's flight of fancy is particularly bizarre:

> Chaque femelle a cinq ou six époux qu'elle emporte parfois dans son vol et qui attendent leur tour, après quoi, rabattus sur le sol, ils y périssent au bout de quelques heures. L'épouse fécondée descend, cherche un gîte dans l'herbe, décroche ses quatre ailes qui tombent à ses pieds comme une robe de noce à la fin de la fête, brosse son corselet et se met a creuser le sol afin de se cloîtrer dans une chambre souterraine et de tenter d'y fonder une colonie nouvelle.
>
> La fondation de cette colonie qui bien souvent n'aboutit qu'au désastre est l'un des épisodes les plus pathétiques et les plus héroiques de la vie des insectes.
>
> Celle qui sera peut-être la mère d'un innombrable peuple, s'enfonce donc dans la terre et s'y façonne une étroite prison. Elle ne possède d'autres vivres que ce qu'elle porte dans son corps, c'est-à-dire, dans le jabot social, une petite provision de rosée miellée, sa chair et ses muscles, surtout les puissants muscles de ses ailes sacrifiées qui seront entièrement résorbées. Rien ne pénètre dans sa tombe qu'un peu d'humidité provenant des pluies et peut-être des mystérieux effluves dont on ignore encore la nature. Patiemment elle attend que s'accomplisse l'oeuvre secrète. Enfin quelques oeufs se répandent autour d'elle. Bientôt, de l'un d'eux, sort une larve qui tisse son cocon, d'autres oeufs s'ajoutent aux premiers, deux ou trois larves en émergent. Qui les nourrit? Ce ne peut

être que la mère puisque la cellule est fermée à tout, hors à l'humidité. Voilà cinq ou six mois qu'elle est enterrée, elle n'en peut plus, elle n'est plus qu'une squelette. Alors commence l'horrible tragédie. Près de mourir d'une mort qui anéantirait du même coup tout l'avenir qui se prépare, elle se résoud à dévorer un ou deux de ses oeufs, ce qui lui donne la force d'en pondre trois ou quatre, ou bien elle se résigne a croquer une des larves, ce qui lui permet, grâce aux apports impondérables dont nous ne connaissons pas la substance, d'en élever et d'en nourrir deux autres; et ainsi, d'infanticides en enfantements, et d'enfantements en infanticides, trois pas en avant, deux pas en arrière, mais avec un gain régulier sur la mort, le funèbre drame se déroule durant près d'une année, jusqu'à ce que se forment deux ou trois petites ouvrières débiles parce que mal nourries depuis l'oeuf, qui perceront les murs de l'*In Pace* ou plutôt de l'*In Dolore*, et iront au dehors chercher les premiers vivres qu'elles rapporteront à leur mère. A partir de ce moment celle-ci ne travaille plus, ne s'occupe plus de rien et nuit et jour, jusqu'à la mort, ne fera plus que pondre. Les temps héroiques sont révolus, l'abondance et la prosperité se prennent la place de la longue famine, la prison se dilate et devient une ville qui d'année en année se répand sous le sol; et la nature ayant mis fin sur ce point a l'un de ses jeux les plus cruels et les moins explicables, s'en va plus loin répéter les mêmes expériences dont nous ne comprenons pas encore la morale ni l'utilité.[30]

My idea for the story was fairly simple. A young scientist marries the daughter of an old clergyman-collector and becomes trapped in a country house which turns out to resemble an antheap, in that it is uncertain whether the source of authority is the incessantly childbearing females or the brisk sexless workers. For a long time I had only these three characters in my head – the Lydgate-like young man, the Farebrother-like old man, and the fecund daughter, who was always associated in my mind with Austen's Lady Bertram. My idea for the film was that the screen would be able to interweave the images of the two communities – ants and people – so as at once to reinforce the analogy and to do the opposite – to show the insects as Other, resisting our metaphorical impositions. I decided quite early to make my hero an Amazon explorer from the lower middle classes like Wallace and Bates and Spruce. I called him William and the old collector Harald out of a blatant reference to Scott's historical vision of old and new rulers, Saxon and Norman. I called the eldest daughter Eugenia, because she was well-born and because the story was something to do with Sexual Selection as well as Natural Selection. Much later in my thinking I saw that I needed another woman, not confined to her biological identity, and invented Matilda – who masquerades through the early part of the story as Matty Crompton, a kind of governessy poor relation, making herself useful in the schoolroom.

Then, as with the other story, I read. Ants, bees, Amazon travels, Darwin, books about Victorian servant life, butterflies and moths – resisting, rather than searching out useful metaphors, but nevertheless finding certain recurring patterns. For instance the Amazonian explorers' use of the imagery of Paradise, which to Wallace in South America was an English field and hedgerow, but in England became the openness of the native people of Brazil and the fecundity of the virgin forest. Knowledge of both places unsettled the images of both, in terms of the Other. I had called William 'Adamson', as a kind of ironic reference to the first man in the first Garden. I discovered quite late in my work the full beauties of the Linnaean system of naming the lepidoptera.

> Linnaeus found a treasure-house of names in the Greek and Roman literature which formed the basis of contemporary education. For the swallowtails he turned to Homer and especially the *Iliad*. He applied the names of Trojan heroes to those that had the thorax marked with red, starting with Priamus, king of Troy. The names of Greek heroes (Achivi) were given to those that lacked this red, headed appropriately enough by Helena 'the face that launched a thousand ships' and her rightful husband Menelaus . . .
>
> After the Equites or Knights came the Heliconi which took their names from the Muses and graces that dwelt on Mt Helicon. The third section are the Danai. Danaus conveniently had fifty daughters, a splendid source for names . . .

The Nymphales follow, and . . . after the Nymphales we have the Plebeji or Commoners (the smaller butterflies).[31]

I thought this was a strange and innocent form of colonialism – the Englishmen wandering through the Virgin Forest in pursuit of creatures called Menelaus and Helen, Apollo and the Heliconiae, and all the Danaides. I was particularly pleased when I discovered in Bates – long after the name of my character was settled – a passage about the *Morphos* – the large blue butterflies – and discovered that there was one called *Morpho Eugenia* (a congener of *Morpho Menelaus* and *Morpho Rhetenor*, according to Bates).[32] I was even more pleased when I discovered elsewhere that Morpho is one of the ways of naming Aphrodite Pandemos, the earthly Venus. I was pleased in the way one is when one *discovers* a myth still alive and working, despite the fact that part of my intention was to undo anthropomorphic imaginings and closures – for reasons akin to those Doris Lessing gives to Anna Wulf, criticising her psychoanalyst for closing off thought with mythic 'wholeness'.

A characteristic of working out a story through the metaphors, and the metaphors through the story, is that you have repeated moments when you discover *precisely* and intellectually something that you always knew instinctively. (Though the story calls in question any definition of instinct.) In this case I realised I was working towards a conversation between Harald who was writing a book on Design in a universe that he accepts is accurately described by Darwin, and William, who is a Darwinian agnostic. Harald uses the arguments of Asa Gray, the Harvard biologist[33] – including Gray's quotation of the places where Darwin still talks of the Works of the Creator, in his description of the development of the eye,[34] and the places where Darwin is led to personify Natural Selection as a kind of Dame Nature. Harald is concerned with the origin of ethical values, and tries to deduce God, the Father of a Family, from human love. (He also uses the arguments used by Charles Kingsley, about God the embryologist, revealed in psalm 139.) William retorts that argument by analogy is only what Feuerbach said it was, projection of the human being to fill the Universe. *Homo Homini Deus est*. Harald answers that it is just as much of an error to suppose that we are no more than automata, on the analogy of the way some naturalists look at insects. This too is dangerous analogy.

William is gloomy, since he is coming to see himself in terms of the male inhabitants of the hive or the anthill. (He would; I made him so; this is a fable.) I felt as though I had found out for the first time that this story, Darwinian, Linnaean, Amazonian, is just as much about analogy, the body, and its sexual functions as *The Conjugial Angel* was. When Matty Crompton talks William into beginning to engineer his release from bondage by writing the history of the local colonies of wood ants (a person more preoccupied with slavery and colonialism would have made a quite different metaphorical structure from these natural-historical facts from the one I made) he finds a metaphor for the flight of the males which I particularly liked – and stitched together from a precise description in a modern naturalist's study.[35]

> And the males too have become specialised, as factory-hands are specialised *hands* for the making of pin-heads or brackets. Their whole existence is directed *only* to the nuptial dance and the fertilisation of the Queens. Their eyes are huge and keen. Their sexual organs, as the fatal day approaches, occupy almost the whole of their body. They are flying amorous projectiles, truly no more than the burning arrows of the winged and blindfold God of Love.

I added both the economic allusion to Adam Smith on specialisation, an allusion to Coleridge's objections to the synechdoche of 'hands' for human beings, and the mythological reference to the burning arrows of the God of Love.

One of the most peculiar aspects of analogy in the study of the Natural world is mimicry – not the mimicry of the poisonous pharmacophages by the edible, but the walking metaphor visible possibly only to humans. (Though bee orchids are metaphors or parodies visible to bees.) We see eyes in the wing-spots of butterflies, we see the deaths-head on the hawk-moth, and we recognise the mask of the bluff attitude of the Elephant Hawk-Moth and the Puss Moth. Very late in the writing of my story I was flicking through my insect book and saw these, and thought they were, so to speak, walking analogies, walking metaphors.

I discovered Colonel Maitland Emmett also very late in the writing of this story. When I read his accounts of the naming of *Deilephila elpenor* and *Cerura vinula*[36] – both of which, by pure chance, were named by Thomas Mouffet, whom I had wanted to 'fit in' and couldn't – I suddenly had the form for the story written by Matty/Matilda under the title 'Things are not what they seem'. At the narrative level this was a veiled warning to William not to suppose that she herself was a sexless worker, and also an even more veiled warning about the relations of his wife with her brother Edgar. But it rapidly turned out to be another metaphor about metaphor-making. It is the story of Seth (Adam's late-born son in Genesis) who is shipwrecked and trapped by a kind of monstrous Marie-Antoinette-like shepherdess called Dame Cottitoe Pan Demos who turns the crew into swine. All this mythology sprang from the discovery that Mouffet had named the snouted caterpillar of the Elephant Hawk-Moth for Odysseus' companion who was turned into a swine by Circe. Seth is rescued by an ant and let out into a walled garden, where he meets Mistress Mouffet, the Spy or Recorder, and the two false dragons, the caterpillars of *Deilephila elpenor* and *Cerura vinula*. Mistress Mouffet helps him to escape on the back of *Sphinx atropos acherontis*, the Death's-Head Hawk-Moth, and he travels to see 'a more powerful Fairy' than Dame Cottitoe. She is in a veiled cavern, has a face like a fierce lion and a beautiful woman, and is spinning continuous gold thread like a cocoon. She asks him a riddle which he answers – 'What is my name?' He stammers out that he does not know, but she must be kind, he thinks she is kind. It was only at this point in my narrative that I realised that I had 'found' another of my own most powerful recurring figures, just as inevitable as Nous/Hyle. She was Spenser's Dame Nature, who 'hath both kinds in one' – and whom I need as I need Sophia and Lilith as images of the female Creator.

> Then forth issewed (great goddesse) great Dame *Nature*,
> With goodly port and gracious Maiesty;
> Being far greater and more tall of stature
> Than any of the gods or Powers on hie:
> Yet certes by her face and physnomy,
> Whether she man or woman inly were
> That could not any creature well descry:

For with a veil that wimpled every where,
Her head and face was hid, that mote to none appeare.

That some doe say was so by skill devised,
To hide the terror of her uncouth hew,
From mortal eyes that should be sore agrized:
For that her face did like a Lion shew,
That eye of wight could not indure to view;
But others tell that it so beautious was
And round about such beames of splendour threw
That it the Sunne a thousand times did pass,
Ne could be seene, but like an image in a glass.[37]

And the rather didactic, Kingsley-like fairy tale, which was a message from Matty to William, had managed to amalgamate Tennyson's statue of Truth 'behind the veil, behind the veil' with the personified Nature of *In Memoriam* LV

> Are God and Nature then at strife
> That Nature sends such fearful dreams?
> So careful of the type she seems
> So careless of the single life.

In the fairy tale Kind sends Seth back with a moth (a genuine one) called Morpheus Caradris to freeze Dame Cottitoe and her retinue with dream-dust – Morpheus, the god of Dreams is also called Phobetor, the terrifier, and shares his 'morph-' root with *Aphrodite pandemos* as *Morpho* because he is a shape-changer. I realised unexpectedly that from the beginning I had set up *Morpho Eugenia*, the aphrodisiac butterfly of sexual selection against Matty, the Sphinx, the night-flyer, who 'hath both kinds in one', lion and woman, and sets and answers the riddle William must solve to be free – sending him an anagram, insect/incest in a word-game. And I was back at the personification problem, because she is also Darwin's Nature, whom the language and the culture led him to personify when what he was telling us about the natural world required him not to, not to posit a Designer, or a Parent.

The problem for the writer, for me, is to do with Wallace Stevens's great line in *Notes Towards a Supreme Fiction*,

> To find, not to impose
> It is possible, possible possible. It must be
> Possible.

Recent theories of language have presented it as a self-referring system with no necessary connection to any part of the world other than our bodies which form it. Writers like Gabriel Josipovici have analysed the Demon of Analogy – the sense that what we thought was Out There and Other is only a description of the inside of our own skulls.[38] That is why I was so suspicious of McLuhan's wish to push Hallam and Tennyson's sensuous images into *paysage intérieur*. We need to look at the *exterior*. One can use studies of ant societies to think about ants, or about ant altruism, or about human altruism. (Maeterlinck, for example, has the most gloomy and beautiful description of the inhuman functionalism of socialist communities through the analogy with termites.) I like the formal *energy* of the relations between Swedenborg's Divine Human and Hallam's insatiable love of God in *The Conjugial Angel*, and the personifications in *Morpho Eugenia* – Venus, Ant Queen, Dame Kind, Matilda. I think the stories are studies of the danger of thinking with images that think with images themselves (like Derrida's *La Métaphore Blanche*) and I do think that in some curious way they find, not impose.

· 5 ·

Old Tales, New Forms

In 1990 I was chairman of the judges for the first presentation of the European Literature prize. I had spent eleven years teaching English and American Literature, and I was curious about what went on in the contemporary Europe of which I, and my writing, were also a part. I can remember the moment when I realised I had discovered a pattern of forms and ideas new at least to me – and at the same time as old as Western literature. I began to read Roberto Calasso's *Le Nozze di Cadmo e Armonia* late one night in bed in the summer on a French mountainside. I was still reading at dawn, hanging over the edge of the bed, and what I was reading was something I already knew – the Greek myths retold at a gallop, sensuous and immediate, and at the same time threaded through with brilliant and knotty reflections on the relations of myth, story, language and reality.

Looking at the other books that excited me amongst the entries I began to discern a general European interest in storytelling, and in thinking about storytelling. There was the Austrian Christoph Ransmayr's *Die Letzte Welt* – a tale set ambivalently in the ancient and modern worlds, of a search for the exiled Ovid, in which the tales of the *Metamorphoses* are retold in a Black Sea iron town. There was the Basque Atxaga's *Obabakoak*, which is a compendium of linked tales, ancient, modern, plagiarised, mirrored, full of energy and invention, reflecting on the absence of a Basque Literature and the need to invent one. There was Gesualdo Bufalino's *Le Menzogne della Notte*, in which a group of condemned conspirators in an island fortress spend the night telling the tales of their lives. There was also Hans Magnus

Enzensberger's *Ach Europa*, not at first sight connected to ancient storytelling, since it is a kind of political travel book about the edges of Europe, the unconsidered parts – but it felt to me, with its chain of connected and disconnected cultural anecdotes, its jigsaw-like *bricolage*, to be somehow part of what I was looking at. I began to think myself about storytelling, about the irrepressible life of old stories.

Some of this interest in storytelling is to do with doubts about the classic novel, with its interest in the construction of the Self, and the relation of that Self to the culture, social and political, surrounding it. A writer can rebel in various ways against the novel of sensibility, or the duty (often imposed by literary journalists) to report on, to criticise, contemporary actuality. You can write anti-novels, like the *nouveau roman*, deconstructing narrative and psychology. Or you can look back at forms in which stories are not about *inner* psychological subtleties, and truths are not connected immediately to contemporary circumstances. There are the great compendious storytelling collections. The *Arabian Nights*, Boccaccio's *Decameron*, the *Canterbury Tales*, Ovid's *Metamorphoses*. The fairy-tale collections of the Brothers Grimm, and Moe and Asbjørnsen in Norway. Sade's *Les Cent Vingt Journées de Sodome* used the Boccaccian form of a group of secluded narrators – in his case inspired to act out the voluptuous and appalling imaginings suggested by the tales. Jan Potocki's *The Saragossa Manuscript* is a fantastic collection of tales within tales within tales, of Muslims, gypsies, a French soldier, Spanish grandees, ghouls and houris during the Napoleonic wars. There is the wonderful collection of Italian folk tales made by Italo Calvino, and there are the literary tales written by Hoffmann, Tieck, and Hans Andersen. Both Angela Carter and Salman Rushdie in Britain in the 1970s said that they felt their energy derived more from reading tales than from reading novels, and used tales, old, invented and reinvented, to charm, to entice and to galvanise their readers in turn. I want to look at some of the ways in which these old tales and forms have had a continued, metamorphic life.

Calvino says (*à propos* of Dante and Galileo) that there is

> a deep-rooted vocation in Italian literature . . . the notion of the literary work as a map of the world and the knowable, of writing driven on by a thirst for knowledge that may by turns

be theological, speculative, magical, encyclopaedic, or may be concerned with natural philosophy or with transfiguring visionary observation. It is a tradition that exists in all European literatures, but I would say that in Italian literature it has been dominant in every shape and form, making our literature very different from others, very difficult but at the same time perfectly unique.[1]

Both Calvino and Calasso are interested in the network of story and myth in this Italian way. Both write and rewrite stories interspersed with erudite and brilliant commentaries on what they are doing. Both tell stories which are commentaries on storytelling.

Calasso's three books, *The Marriage of Cadmus and Harmony*, *The Ruin of Kasch*, and *Ka* are three parts of what he sees as one work, about the origins in myth and ritual of both storytelling and political institutions. Calasso sees human history in terms of an increasing distance between the divine and the human, in which myth succeeds sacrifice, and stories succeed myths. Myths, like organic life, are shape-shifters, metamorphic, endlessly reconstituted and reformed. He begins *The Marriage* with the myth of Europa and the bull.

Stories never live alone: they are the branches of a family that we have to trace back, and forward. In the rapture of her sea crossing on the back of a white bull, Europa conceals within herself, like still undiscovered powers, the destinies of her love-crazed granddaughters Phaedra and Ariadne, who would one day hang themselves out of shame and desperation. And down among the celestial roots of this story tree we come across the wanderings of the mad heifer, the ancestral Io, who again holds within herself the image of another mad heifer, mother of Phaedra and Ariadne: Pasiphaë. And she too hung herself in shame.

Calasso links the development of stories in stories to metamorphosis.

Forms would become manifest insofar as they underwent metamorphosis. Each form had its own perfect sharpness, so long as it retained that form, but everybody knew that a moment later it might become something else. At the time of

Europa and Io the veil of epiphany was still operating. The
bellowing bull, the crazed cow, would once again appear as god
and girl. But as generation followed generation, metamorphosis became more difficult, and the fatal nature of
reality, its irreversibility, all the more evident.[2]

Irreversibility. Nemesis. Much later in his book Calasso returns to
the connection between the two, describing Zeus's rape of Nemesis
herself, who

> fled to the ends of the earth, transforming herself into one
> animal after another, just as the manifest flees and scatters
> before being caught and pinned down by its principle. The
> same sequence of flight with metamorphoses followed by rape
> is repeated when Peleus chases Thetis and finally couples with
> her in the form of a cuttlefish. The repetition of a mythical
> event, with its play of variations, tells us that something
> remote is beckoning to us. There is no such thing as the
> isolated mythical event, just as there is no such thing as the
> isolated word. Myth, like language, gives all of itself in each of
> its fragments. When a myth brings into play repetition and
> variants, the skeleton of the system emerges for a while, the
> latent order, covered in seaweed.

And Calasso goes on to divide the world into four 'realms' –

> perennial metamorphosis, that of every beginning when the
> word has not yet detached itself from the thing, nor the mind
> from the matter; the realm of substitution is the world of the
> digit, above all the sign, the digit as sign, as incessant
> substitution; the realm of the unique is the world that always
> eludes the clutches of language, the very appearing of the
> irrepeatable; the realm of Zeus is that of the Greek stories, of
> which we are still a part.[3]

Calasso chose the marriage of Cadmus and Harmony as the focus of his
book because it was, according to him, the last occasion on which the
gods sat down to share a feast with mortals, and because Cadmus
invented writing, invented the sign which, substituted for the thing,

made myths into stories. On the edge of myth, he says, is Odysseus, who also wrote, and who tells more stories than any other mythic hero. Told stories are a step away from the epiphany and written stories are further still. Calasso is a Nietzsche scholar, and like Nietzsche he desires a culture with 'a horizon ringed about with myths'.[4] He writes brilliantly of the 'wonderful flatness of the Homeric vision' in which gods and daimons were the same, as were men and heroes. And he loves the Greeks – 'unique among the Mediterranean peoples' for not passing on their stories through a priestly authority. 'In Greece myth escapes from ritual like a genie from a bottle.' 'If the stories start to become independent, to develop names and relationships, then one day you realise they have taken on a life of their own.'[5]

In *The Ruin of Kasch*, a tale of European legitimacy and self-consciousness that begins with Talleyrand, and wanders through Marx and Durkheim, the secret services and Nazism, he tells the tale of Kasch between chapters on the Port-Royal and on Law and Order. The tale is of a successful kingdom where the priests read the stars, and when they saw the appointed time, they strangled the king and appointed his successor. Then a storyteller came from the distant East, and told stories, and the king decreed that he should tell stories until the day of sacrifice and die with the king. But a woman storyteller came, and persuaded the storyteller to desire to live happily, and the priests to listen to the stories all night, instead of looking at the order of the heavens, and so they lost their connection to the order of things, and fell dead. And the king and the two storytellers lived happily, but the power of the kingdom declined, and it was invaded. This tale is a tale of legitimacy derived from ritual, and decadence connected with storytelling substituted for myth. 'The ruin of Kasch is the origin of literature,' says Calasso, who also, like Nietzsche, sees the Platonic dialogue as the origin of the novel, a discursive individual form. 'Mythical figures live many lives, die many deaths, and in this they differ from the characters we find in novels who can never go beyond the single gesture.'[6] Nietzsche in *The Birth of Tragedy* writes with nostalgia of Homer's capacity to *see* both his people and the images he uses. This immediacy is Schiller's naïve poetry, as opposed to the feelings and thought of sentimental poems. Calasso tells his Greek tales with a Homeric immediacy and meditates on them with a Nietzschean subtlety and directness.

Calasso's story of the stories begins with epiphany. Calvino, in an essay called 'Cybernetics and Ghosts', tells his own story of the stories, which begins with the invention of language and codes. The storyteller invented patterns to explain the world with a limited number of figures – 'jaguar, coyote, toucan, piranha, father, son, brother-in-law, uncle, wife, mother, sister, mother-in-law'. These performed a limited number of actions, 'they could be born, marry, die, copulate, sleep, fish, hunt, climb trees, dig burrows, eat and defecate, make prohibitions, transgress them, steal or give away fruit and other things – things that were also classified in a limited catalogue'. This is a Lévi-Straussian vision of coded words and narratives. Myth, according to this tale, broke in with the indescribable.

> The storyteller of the tribe puts together phrases and images: the younger son gets lost in the forest, he sees a light in the distance, he walks and walks; the fable unwinds from sentence to sentence, and where is it leading? To the point at which something not yet said, something as yet only darkly felt by presentiment, suddenly appears and seizes us and tears us to pieces, like the fangs of a man-eating witch. Through the forest of fairy-tale the vibrancy of myth passes like a shudder of wind.[7]

In Calvino's story, the secrecy and silence of myth, which needs to be controlled by ritual, and creates the unconscious in humans, come *after* storytelling.

> Until now it has generally been said that the fable is a 'profane' story, something that comes after myth, a corruption or vulgarization or secularization of it, or that fable and myth coexist and counterbalance each other as different functions of a single culture. The logic of my argument however . . . leads to the conclusion that the making of fables precedes the making of myths. Mythic significance is something one comes across only if one persists in playing around with narrative functions.[8]

Calvino is interested both in patterns like grammar, maths, cybernetics, chemistry, and in narrative. In his preface to his wonderful collection of 'Fiabe' – tales, fables – he describes the recurrent motifs, and repeatedly uses the metaphor of a 'network' to which I shall return. But at the same time he feels, quite as immediately and violently as Calasso, the attraction of the immediacy and reality of the stories. Once he had finished the book, he wrote, he realised that his work had confirmed something he had suspected, or partly known *'ed è che io credo questo: le fiabe sono vere'*. The reasons for the truth of the tales is the human truths they reiterate plainly – the fate of beauty and ugliness, fear and hope, chance and disaster. Like Calasso, Calvino, elsewhere, insists on the primary importance of the tale, or the myth, as told, the story itself not this or that ascribed meaning or interpretation. In the first of his *Six Memos for the Next Millennium*, 'Lightness', he tells the tale of Perseus, carefully and gently resting the dead head of the Medusa on seaweeds which turn to coral.

> With myths, one should not be in a hurry. It is better to let them settle in the memory, to stop and dwell on every detail, to reflect on them without losing touch with their language of images. The lesson we can learn from a myth lies in the literal narrative, not in what we add to it from the outside.[9]

And in an essay on Ovid, he discusses the possible interpretations of the fable of Arachne – was Athene justified in punishing sacrilege, was Arachne a poet in the image of Ovid himself – and answers himself : 'Neither the one nor the other. In the vast catalogue of myths that the entire poem in fact is, the myth of Athena and Arachne may in its turn contain two smaller catalogues aimed in opposing ideological directions: one to induce holy terror, the other to incite people to irreverence and moral relativity.' The author of the *Metamorphoses* gives a place to 'all the stories or implied stories that flow in every direction . . . to be sure of presenting no partial design but rather a living multiplicity that excludes no god known or unknown'.[10]

Immediacy, polymorphy. The reason Calvino gives for his professional interest, *as a writer*, in the traditional fairy tale, comes, in the *Six Memos*, under 'Quickness'. He is interested in the tales, not because of any connection to a national culture (he is urban and modern) nor as a result of childhood nostalgia (he was brought up on science books) but *formally*. He likes the economy, the rhythm and the hard logic of the tales, he says, the stories within stories that show the relativity of time, what he calls the 'laconic' tone of them. And it is these formal qualities, I think, that link those European works I see as connected to the old stories and the old ways of telling.

The novel in the nineteenth and twentieth centuries has always incorporated forms of myths and fairy tales, working both with and against them. Fanny Price *is* Cinderella, and Gwendolen Harleth in *Daniel Deronda* is named for a Celtic goddess, and comes embellished (and metamorphosed) by references to snake-women, La Motte-Fouqué's Undine and Goethe's Melusine. Thomas Mann built modern novels around the Faust legend and the Venusberg, and *Ulysses* is misleadingly famous for using the old myths to 'order' the random chaos and fragmentation of modern life. Jungian thought finds archetypes 'deep' in individual characters – the virgin, the mother and the crone, or the Double. Psychoanalysis, as has often been pointed out, is a narrative. Myths and fairy stories can be recuperated from dreams and interpreted in the way in which Freud interpreted dreams. Calvino remarks somewhere that Bruno Bettelheim's account of the fairy tales is hermeneutic in a simple way, seeing the tales as allegories of personal development – the Sleeping Beauty is the drowsiness of adolescent and pubescent girls. Doris Lessing's Anna Wulf in *The Golden Notebook* refers to her analyst, whom she nicknames Mother Sugar, as a 'witch-doctor' and is irritated by Mother Sugar's satisfaction when Anna brings her a dream of 'joy-in-destruction' personified as a spiteful little old man. Anna remarks shrewdly that this understanding does nothing to change the mess she is in in the 'real' world of the 'realist' story she is living.[11] Freud and Jung produce hermeneutics and 'depth', not the quickness and lightness, the laconic narration and irreducibility that entrance Calvino.

I have myself become increasingly interested in quickness and lightness of narrative – in small discrete stories rather than pervasive and metamorphic metaphors as ways of patterning and thinking out a text. When I wrote *The Virgin in the Garden* in the 1960s and 70s I *discovered* a kind of ruling myth and meaning in the metaphors I was using instinctively, which derived in part from studying Elizabeth I's mythologising of herself as Virgin Queen, Cynthia, Diana, Astraea.

The book began moral – its working title was 'A Fugitive Virtue' from Milton's *Areopagitica* – and ended intricately layered and mythic. By the time I wrote *Possession* in the 1980s my interest in both character and narration had undergone a change – I felt a need to *feel and analyse* less, to tell more flatly, which is sometimes more mysteriously. The real interest of this to a writer is partly in the intricacies of the choice of words from line to line. I found myself crossing out psychological descriptions, or invitations to the reader to enter the characters' thought-process. I found myself using stories within stories, rather than shape-shifting recurrent metaphors, to make the meanings. One example is the use I made of the very conventional tale of the man choosing between three women – the choice of Paris or the Three Caskets scene in *The Merchant of Venice*, about which Freud wrote so beautifully and suggestively. Freud says the three women are always a man's mother, his wife, and Death, and he compares Lear's third daughter, Cordelia, to the Valkyrie of the battlefield. I wrote a chapter called 'The Threshold' in which a wandering Childe meets three fairies, gold, silver and leaden, who offer him power, sex, and mystery. I wrote it in the arch Victorian narrative voice of my Victorian heroine, who would rather that he had chosen the golden lady, but knew he must follow the leaden one under the arch of the standing stones into fairyland or the underworld. I set this tale between the modern campus-novel narrative and the calling up of the ghosts of the Victorian poets in their rediscovered love-letters. The pleasure of writing it was in handling the old, worn counters of the characterless persons, the Fate of the consecutive events, including the helpless commentary of the writer on the unavoidable grip of the story, and a sense that I was myself partaking in the continuity of the tales by retelling them in a new context in a way old and new. Christabel's commentary was 'knowing' about inevitability; my own writing was 'knowing' about Freud. But the *story* was primary and had its own life.

I thought vaguely – or rather felt – that an interest in tales is something the young have, and the ageing rediscover. Analysis of motives and responsibilities is for the middle years when human beings are in the middle of decision-making and choosing partners. I wrote a tale called *The Djinn in the Nightingale's Eye* as a tale about this

discovery. My heroine is an ageing narratologist, who finds a Djinn in
a glass bottle in a hotel room in Istanbul. It is stories within stories
again – the Djinn and the woman tell each other their lives, as lovers
do on meeting, the woman tells tales at conferences as examples, and
so on. I knew when I began that the Djinn himself figured both death
as an invigorating force, and also the passion for reading tales.
Children read stories as though they themselves are infinite and
immortal. The old read tales knowing that they themselves are finite,
that the tales will outlive them. The Djinn is immortal, as the tales are.
At one point my heroine (who has an Alice-in-Wonderland English
empirical stubbornness) realises that both the many-breasted Diana of
Ephesus and the Djinn are more real than she herself, in her mortal and
fragile body. More people have known and have believed in the
goddess than will ever believe in her. I connect my great pleasure in
this perception to the pleasure I felt, when, after a momentary
irritation at finding that Iris Murdoch had just published a working of
the Marsyas story I was working with myself, I understood that the tales
had power because they were alive everywhere. A myth derives force
from its endless repeatability. 'Originality' and 'individuality', those
novelistic aesthetic necessities, were neither here nor there.

So I stumbled, whilst working, across the idea that stories and tales,
unlike novels, were intimately to do with death. During the height of
the *nouveau roman*'s opposition to storytelling, which was preceded by
the modernist desire for the timeless epiphany, those who believed in
narrative were pointing out, like Michel Butor, that we are narrative
beings because we live in biological time. Whether we like it or not,
our lives have beginnings, middles and ends. We narrate ourselves to
each other in bars and beds. Walter Benjamin,[12] in his essay on 'The
Storyteller' points out that a man's life becomes a story at the point of
death. He instances the life that flashes before the eyes of a drowning
man, the required death-bed confession, the way the mourners start
narrating the dead, from the moment of death onwards. The classic
collections of tales can be described in the words Malcolm Bowie[13]
takes from Proust's comparison of *A La Recherche* to the *Arabian Nights*,
as 'big books of death-defying stories'. Scheherazade tells stories to
defer the daily sentence of death. Boccaccio's storytellers have
retreated from Florence to escape the Plague. The first story told in the

Decameron is that of a great sinner whose fraudulent and untruthful death-bed confession – the story as lie – gains him absolution from a credulous friar.

Three European literary tales of great elegance and power – one Danish, one Italian and one Dutch – might illustrate this relation of storytelling and death. (I shall come back to a brief consideration of the literary tale as a genre later.) The Dane is Karen Blixen (Isak Dinesen), the Italian is Gesualdo Bufalino, and the Dutchman is Cees Nooteboom.

Blixen in 'The Cardinal's First Tale', in *Last Tales*, gives an account of the difference between tales and novels. Her Cardinal in this tale is a surviving twin, of a pair named Atanasio and Dionysio, whose parents designed them for the priesthood and the life of the artist respectively. It was not clear which infant had perished in a fire, but the Cardinal sees himself as both in one. He makes a speech to a lady which gives a precise historical description of the relation between the tale and the novel.

> 'Madame,' he said, 'I have been telling you a story. Stories have been told as long as speech has existed, and *sans* stories the human race would have perished, as it would have perished *sans* water. You will see the characters of the true story clearly, as if luminous and on a higher plane, and at the same time they may not look quite human, and you may well be a little afraid of them. That is all in the order of things . . . I see today a new art of narration, a novel literature and category of belles-lettres, dawning upon the world . . . And this new art and literature – for the sake of the individual characters in the story, and in order to keep close to them and not be afraid – will be ready to sacrifice the story itself.'

The lady replies that she herself loves the 'live and sympathetic persons of modern novels'. The Cardinal characterises it as 'the literature of individuals, if we may call it so'. It is, he says, 'a noble art, a great, earnest and ambitious human product. But it is a human product. The divine art is the story. In the beginning was the story.' The human characters came, he says on the sixth day only and the day of judgment will be the end of the story.

Whatever he is in himself the immortal story immortalises its hero. Ali Baba, who in himself is no more than an honest woodcutter, is the adequate hero of a very great story. But by the time when the new literature shall reign supreme and you will have no more stories, you will have no more heroes.

The lady is left wondering if the priest or the artist speaks, and also who is the Master he serves. The reader is left with a sense of the archaic – and religious – power of tales in which individual consciousness is not the important thing.

I have already mentioned Bufalino's *Le Menzogne della Notte*. Karen Blixen's *The Deluge at Norderney* is one of her *Seven Gothic Tales* (1934) and thought by many to be her masterpiece. The tale concerns a violent flood that drowns a bathing resort on the west coast of Holstein in 1835. The townspeople rescue the farmers and the rich people from the baths, in boats. The Cardinal, Hamilcar von Sehestedt is particularly heroic. The final boat before dusk passes a farmhouse threatened with submerging, and the Cardinal, a rich mad old spinster called Miss Malin Nat-og-dag (Night and Day), and two young people – a melancholic student and Miss Malin's maid – agree to replace the farm family and see out the night. If the house withstands the waters they can be rescued when daylight comes. During the long night, Miss Nat-og-dag presides over a storytelling, where young and old tell their life-stories. These are Gothic, strange, and turn on illusory identities provided by uncertain genealogies. The Cardinal turns out to be an actor, the bastard son of Philippe-Egalité, who murdered the real Cardinal. Miss Malin is a believer in noble blood, and a virginal fantasist who believes herself to be the greatest courtesan of her time. The young people have been the puppets of the fantasies of their elders, a sensual Count and a homosexual aesthetic uncle. Their tales are full of shadows and glitter, mirrors and pain. Other tales are told, including the false Cardinal's Tale of the encounter of St Peter with Barabbas. The young become lovers, are 'married' by the Cardinal, and sleep in each others' arms; the old maid and the actor discuss masks, bastardy, and grinning back at the devil. The power of the story is in its narrative tension – the presence of the rising waters, the slow approach of the end of the night. Miss Nat-og-dag becomes, in her exhaustion, a figure of Death – 'She had on her shoulders that death's-head by which druggists label their poison bottles, an unengaging object for any man to kiss.' Kasparson, the actor, praises masks and fictions. 'Not by the face shall the man be known but by the mask.' They 'grin back at death' together and kiss solemnly like figures in a Dance of Death. Robert Langbaum[14] believes that we are to read the ending one way – the narrator tells us that the old maid did not go unkissed to her grave, and there is a wonderful image of the rising water, which has soaked her silk skirt, reaching the loft floor. 'A dark figure, like that of a long thick snake, was lying upon the boards, and a little lower down where the floor slanted slightly, it widened to a black pool . . . Indeed, as they moved they felt the heavy boards gently rocking, floating upon the waters.' They then see the dawn through the cracks in the wall. 'Between the boards a strip of fresh deep blue was showing, against which the little lamp seemed to make a red stain.' The title of the tale contains the Biblical word for the Flood, the 'deluge', and it is possible that the little house is the ark, as it is possible that it is a tomb. Blixen's last sentence is a masterly evocation of the whole tradition of storytelling against death.

> The old woman slowly drew her fingers out of the man's hands
> and placed one upon her lips.
> 'A ce moment de sa narration,' she said, 'Scheherazade vit
> paraître le matin, et discrète, se tut.'[15]

Dawn was always Scheherazade's saviour, as well as the threatened moment of her doom. Blixen's splendid tale, like her heroine's name, is double, surely, suggests forking paths of possibility.

Bufalino's much later tale[16] contains many of the same narrative elements. The four conspirators lie in the chapel of the citadel, watching and hearing the building of the scaffold on which they are to die at dawn unless one of them saves all of them by betraying the name of their leader, known as 'God the Father', in a secret ballot. They pass away the night telling their life-stories – the youngest, Narcissus, is in terror of the blade – and, as in Blixen's tale, the movement of time to an end is more powerful than any of the individual characters. As in Blixen's tale too, the stories are partly couched as confessions to what turns out to be a false friar, who is apparently a fellow-prisoner, bloody and battered, but is in fact the prison governor in disguise. The tension of the ballot joins the tension of fear; no one betrays the leader, but the governor believes that the conspirators have inadvertently betrayed his identity as a close member of the ducal family. The coda to the tale is the governor's own suicide note. He has slowly discovered that the life-stories on which he based his information were a tissue of lies – which he himself reinforced, in accusing the putative 'God the Father' with planted 'evidence'. The conspirators went to their death with mocking smiles. Here again, as in Boccaccio, and to an extent in Blixen, death-bed confessions are fakes, lies, made-up stories. These tales are stories about storytelling.

Cees Nooteboom's *The Following Story*[17] is also a collection of stories about and against death. Its narrator, who had gone to bed in Amsterdam, wakes up in Portugal, 'with the ridiculous feeling that I might be dead, but whether I was actually dead, or had been dead, or vice versa, I could not ascertain'. He remembers his life – he has been a teacher of Classics, and a travel writer, under the name of Dr Strabo. The book is in a sense his description of his life reforming itself in his mind as he lies dying or dead. It contains stories, mostly of deaths – his passion is Ovid, and he is given to acting out scenes such as the Death of Phaethon to his classes, and also Plato's account of the death of Socrates. The love of his life is a red-headed Portuguese science teacher, who tells different stories, with slides, of the decay of dead rats and the furious life of maggots and sexton beetles. He remarks to her that 'Death is the never-ending story'. She says, 'I don't know about that. There's sure to be an end at some point. There has to be a beginning too.' Later the narrator finds himself on a boat which has sailed from Belem (Bethlehem) in Lisbon, to Belem at the mouth of the Amazon and is proceeding along the great river with a group of passengers who recite their deaths and disappear. They are strangers to each other, a Chinese professor, an Italian priest, an airline pilot, a child, a journalist, briefly connected. They tell their tales – disparate, brief, moving – and look at the stars and the water. There is a woman there – Mnemosyne, maybe – to whom the stories are told, and who is also the narrator's favourite pupil, 'so young that one could speak about immortality with her. And then I told her, then I told you

The following story.'

This ending, like Blixen's quotation from the Arabian Nights, turns the tale of death into a narrative infinity, since the story becomes circular – except that Nooteboom suggests that after the second telling the consciousness casts off. His tale is full of cross-references, connections, metamorphoses both biological and mythological. It is set in the Lisbon of Pessoa, the poet who was many masks at once.

The Following Story introduces the frame of the journey as a shared space for storytelling, to be added to the confinement, the confessional and the death-sentence. Storytellers may be pilgrims or wanderers – like Chaucer's pilgrims, proceeding towards the shrine of a murdered priest at Canterbury, or Potocki's travellers. For wanderers space is time, and at this point the experience of reading the highly constructed literary web of tales seems to connect with the web of tales held together by topography and anecdote. One beautiful example is W.G. Sebald's *The Emigrants*,[18] a series of brief lives of Jews driven abroad by the events of the second world war, whose deaths come slowly and late, but are nevertheless caused by the events which led to their wanderings, their diaspora. Their will to live peters out like slow waters in an estuary, and all the tales are part of one tale, and have the mystery of being told *from outside* by a narrator piecing together what he can. The form of *The Emigrants* can be compared to the form of Claudio Magris's masterpiece, *Danubio*, a travel book which traces the river from its uncertain source to its mouth, across cultures, histories, nations and peoples, including myths, stories, ancient tales and recent anecdotes. The river is both an arbitrary formal device and a very natural one, embedded in reality, its existence determining the form of human communities (and those of other creatures). Magris's story wanders with its path, telling now of mediaeval battles, now of prehistory, now of world wars and the Austrian empire. His river is the Heraclitean river into which no man steps twice, and it is the River of Life, flowing into the Black Sea where 'even today the power of words projects on to the Black Sea the image of a waste of waters, a vast oppressive pond, a place of exile, of winters and solitudes'. There is Tomis, where Ovid was exiled, and Magris writes of memories of sick Nietzsche, and peoples the bay with gulls crying out 'Medea' and 'Charon's boat launched from a state-owned shipyard'.

With Magris's interest in history and story and metamorphosis, goes an interest, as it does in Calvino and Nooteboom, in natural history, and the creatures. Again and again his brief chapters combine anecdotal biographies with a sense of the relation of human life to the life of the creatures, which is modern, not Ovidian, though both have a sense of the interrelatedness of things. In Part 3, Chapter 13, 'Two-headed Eagle and White-tailed Eagle' he meditates on Marshal Marsili in 1726 describing and listing the fish and the birds of the Danube near Tulln. He describes also the work, centuries later in the same place, of Konrad Lorenz, and remarks that 'the irredeemable woe of animals, that obscure people who follow our existence like a shadow, throws on us the whole weight of original sin'. He admires Lorenz for understanding that 'animals do not merely have comfortable instinctual mechanisms as it is comfortable to believe' and speculates that a naturalist 'is probably of the opinion (like one of Musil's characters) that if God became man he might or ought to become a cat also or a flower'. He then shifts his ground and argues that the same naturalist, not considering the human species to be sacred and absolute, may be led to justify and exalt all kinds of chauvinism, 'the elementary law of the bond of the group which in the heat of the struggle clouds all judgements and values'. Referring to Lorenz's past leanings towards Nazism he comments

> Thus in the end one can accept any sort of violence committed under stress for the solidarity of the group, and the extermination put into effect by the Third Reich ends up by appearing not all that dissimilar or qualitatively different from the immense slaughter of black rats carried out by the brown rats when they invaded Europe in the eighteenth century.

Magris's attitude to Lorenz is opaque and moving. At the end of his journey, moving out into the Delta in a boat, he observes

> Perched on a tree, a cormorant that has opened its wings to dry off is etched against the sky like a crucifix, the gnats swarm like an uncaring handful of the loose coinage of life; and the German scholar who specializes in Danubian literature does not envy Kafka or Musil, with their genius for depicting dark cathedrals or inconclusive committees, but rather Fabre or

Maeterlinck, the bards of the bees and the termites; and he understands how Michelet, having written the history of the French revolution would have liked to write the history of the birds and the sea. Linnaeus is a poet, when he urges us to count the bones of a fish, and the scales of a snake, and to observe and distinguish between the flying-feathers and the steering-feathers of a bird.

He praises the catalogue of the museum of the Delta, and remarks that Linnaeus numbers among scientists not only botanists 'but also the most chancy amateurs, including poets, theologians, librarians and miscellaneous others. But the miscellany is a summary of the world, while all around is the real world . . .'[19]

'The miscellany is a summary of the world, while all around is the real world.' The miscellany is another form of collected storytelling. Magris's journey, like Sebald's – and Sebald's second journey book owes much to Sir Thomas Browne, the miscellanist par excellence – is a miscellany and a summary of the world, like the *Metamorphoses*. Calvino, in the essay on Cybernetics and Ghosts I have already quoted, and also in his essay on 'Ovid and Universal Contiguity' makes some brilliant remarks about that aspect of storytelling which derives from what he calls 'combinatorial games' – art derived from the formal exploration of 'the possibilities of permutation and transmutation implicit in language' as suggested in Gombrich's development of Freud's ideas on word-play and jokes. Calvino refers his readers to an interesting essay in Spanish (1966) by Hans Magnus Enzensberger on what Enzensberger calls 'topological fictions', using the word 'topological' to mean both mathematical game-playing, and narratives constructed with spatial rather than with temporal images. Enzensberger is of course interested in Borges's images of the world as a library or as a labyrinth. The most famous *locus* of that perhaps is the tale of *The Garden of Forking Paths* in which the Chinese Ts'ui Pen constructed an infinite object that was simultaneously a book and a labyrinth. Stephen Albert says to Ts'ui Pen's descendant, the assassin on his trail, that Ts'ui Pen had written : *I leave to several futures (not to all) my garden of forking paths*. He says

Before unearthing this letter, I had wondered how a book could be infinite. The only way I could surmise was that it be a cyclical or circular volume, a volume whose last page would be identical to the first so that one could go on indefinitely. I also recalled that night at the centre of the *1001 Nights* when the queen Scheherazade (through some magical distractedness on the part of the copyist) begins to retell, verbatim, the story of the 1001 Nights, with the risk of returning once again to the night on which she is telling it – and so on *ad infinitum*. I also pictured to myself a Platonic, hereditary sort of work, passed down from father to son, in which each new individual would add a chapter or with reverent care correct his elders' pages.'[20]

He sees that the forking paths are a forking in *time* – but the image is spatial – and the 'chaotic novel' contains several simultaneous futures, in one of which Fang kills the intruder, in another the intruder kills Fang, in one they are enemies, in another friends, and so on. I like the conjunction here of the infinity of Scheherazade's repetitions and the infinity of genetic replication in the 'hereditary sort of work' which fits onto the biological image of the metamorphoses. Enzensberger[21] gives as an example of a topological fiction the German rhyme in which a black dog goes into a kitchen and steals a bone, and the cook kills him with a ladle, after which many black dogs in tears carry him away and bury him under a stone on which they write, 'A black dog went into a kitchen and stole a bone . . . , etc etc. Enzensberger draws a topology of this which is a series of concentric circles. Each retelling is *inside* the original and its predecessors. Linear stories of death carry inside themselves images of infinity, as topologies of infinity carry inside themselves images of death. Fang shoots Albert. Nooteboom's narrator begins by dying and ends at the beginning of the following story. Magris's miscellany is a summary of the world, a taxonomy or topography 'while all around is the real world'. In Potocki's *Saragossa Manuscript* the Wandering Jew's account of his endless travelling is interwoven with the philosophical system of a character called Velasquez, who has a scientific religion based on infinite numbers, Newtonian physics and the endless metamorphoses of organic matter.

This approach through mathematical patternings of possible worlds connects the Calvino who was an associate of Oulipo to the Calvino who wrote on the universal contiguities of Ovid. European storytelling derives great energy from artifice, constraints and patterning. There is Perec's *La Vie, mode d'emploi*, which proceeds through the rooms of an imaginary house in the knight's moves of chess, describing always the same elements in the different tales in the different rooms. There is Calvino's *Castle of Crossed Destinies*, generated from the tarot pack, and Lawrence Norfolk's *Lempriére's Dictionary*, in which his fantastic plot is patterned in episodes drawn from the original dictionary of classical myths.

Tibor Fischer's *The Collector Collector* is an ingenious *jeu d'esprit*, a mixture of a ribald modern narrative and a collection of tales set at varying points in historical and geographical space, narrated by an apparently indestructible and variably metamorphic jar or vase. The title is a kind of *mise-en-abîme*, a verbal repeated circularity. Fischer admires Apuleius, and has a Rabelaisian philosophical gusto and gloom. The English poet, John Fuller is an elegant tale-teller and puzzle-maker. His latest book, *A Skin Diary*, is a biography of a foetus from conception to birth, constructed around the headings of Roget's *Thesaurus*. His *Look Twice* has the device of tale-tellers fleeing death and pretending to be who they are not, in a train fleeing a Revolution in Eastern Europe – pinned against the buffers and under fire, they escape by constructing a balloon from a panoramic image of the city they have left. This would have appealed to Enzensberger's topographical imagination. Fuller's wonderful collection of miscellaneous short tales, *The Worm and the Star*, covers centuries and continents, joining the physical world of space and light to the organic world of life and death (the worm) in a repeated and endlessly varied metaphor. There is the Basque, Bernardo Atxaga's, extraordinary *Obabakoak*, which he himself compares to the ancient board game, the Game of the Goose, *el juego de la oca, le jeu de l'oie, il gioco dell'occa*, with the storyteller Mother Goose on the sixty-third square, and others containing the maze, the prison and death (a skull or a skeleton.) There is Primo Levi's *The Periodic Table*, divided into chapters representing the chemical elements, with narrative brevities and depths which connect it to Sebald's *Emigrants*. Levi the scientist and artist conforms to Calvino's description of the Italian desire to describe the cosmos. His final chapter on the metamorphoses of a carbon element which is rock, tree, flesh, air, sky and the final dot of the manuscript is infinity and death in one wonderful transmutation. And the Irish poet,

Ciaran Carson, has just published (1999) *Fishing for Amber: A Long Story*. This beautiful, intricate and original miscellany has chapters with alphabetical headings, from Antipodes to Zoetrope, each of which, using the metaphor of amber, matter trapped in translucent fossilised gum, combines tales from Ovid, Irish fairy stories and images and tales of Dutch culture in the Golden Age of Vermeer and Rembrandt.

I have talked about myth, fairy tale, anecdote, miscellany and pattern-making. I should also say something about the relation of the contemporary stories I am interested in to the selfconsciously *literary* tale, both in earlier centuries and now. I know a professional storyteller who tells his own versions of Gilgamesh and Grimm – he believes passionately that literary stories, with authors and deliberate artifice are not part of the fund of myth and folk tale which can be told. Benjamin,[22] too, is disparaging of 'the "short story" which has removed itself from oral tradition and no longer permits that slow piling one on top of the other of thin transparent layers which constitute the most appropriate picture of the way in which the perfect narrative is revealed through the layers of a variety of retellings'. I don't think the writers are purist about the sources of tales in quite this way. Calvino and Bufalino are quite deliberately – in works like *The Baron in the Trees*, *The Cloven Viscount* and the *Non-existent Knight* – reverting to the philosophical tale of the late eighteenth and early nineteenth centuries. Rousseau and Diderot are there as well as the Italian fables and Ovid, as is the Gothic of the early Romantics. Italian literature and German literature do not have a tradition of the powerful social novel that flourished in France, Russia and Britain, and writers feeling frustrated and confined by social realism can turn to Goethe's tales, Tieck and Hoffmann, as well as the brothers Grimm.

I mentioned Angela Carter and Rushdie talking of their sense of the life of tales as opposed to novels. I was teaching in an art school in the sixties, and had many students who were passionate about Tolkien, fairy tales and even Beatrix Potter but could not or would not read novels with social density. I remember my own first experience of the idea that it was possible – and exhilarating – to write tales and not social studies came earlier than Carter's remarks, from reading Karen Blixen. Robert Langbaum's 1964 study of her work, *The Gayety of*

Vision, has an epigraph from Thomas Mann on Freud and the Future, and is in part a polemical defence of her tales as serious literature in a post-Leavisian world. But I experienced them as a liberation, a fresh wind from wherever I had started reading and imagining. She herself expressed enthusiasm for E.T.A. Hoffmann and was much influenced by Kleist's essay on marionettes. Danish literature too, I am told, has no great tradition of realist fiction, and its great writer is Hans Andersen. Blixen saw a similarity between Andersen and Voltaire, and felt herself to be alone in this until she found an entry by Andersen himself, in a Dictionary of Contemporaries in French, saying 'Avec un esprit qui rappelle celui de M. Voltaire Andersen a tout le sentiment des peuples du Nord.'[23] In the cases of both Calvino and Blixen, the narrative drive, and the use of fantasy, of highly sophisticated literary tales have given rise to new forms. I am much less happy about a great many resolute feminist rewritings of fairy tales, making wilful changes to plots and forms to show messages of female power (often written under the enthusiastic misapprehension that fairy tales in general show powerless females). The philosophical tale is one thing. The tale with allegorical, or political designs on the reader is another. (This is also true in the case of Andersen himself when not at his best.)

Another combination of ancient forms and modern stories which is only at the edge of my present concern is the insertion of a reworked myth into a modern novel – not as Mann or Proust or Joyce did, for these novels are barer, simpler, more like tales than those – but still novels. I am thinking of Ransmayr's *Die Letzte Welt* where somehow the reworked Ovidian equivalents have too much novelistic character, too little surprising variability to be pure tale-telling. It is between novel and tale, a form of its own, but not quite what I am talking about. Another novel in this category is *The File on H*, Ismail Kadare's delightful tale of two Irish-American scholars looking for the roots of Homeric oral narrative in the recitations of Albanian rhapsodes. Their tape-recordings are destroyed by an angry hermit under the influence of a jealous Serbian nationalist priest. The narrative is conducted in various styles, from bureaucratic reports of spies to segments of bloody epics, and the romantic fantasies of the governor's wife, a would-be Helen. Their defeat is their victory, for the episode of the destruction of the 'Aprath' (German *Apparat*, tape-recorder) becomes part of a new epic. *The Palace of Dreams*, Kadare's allegorical fantasy about a secret Ministry of Dreams, is also more a novel than a form inspired by the *Thousand and One Nights* to which it is nevertheless related.

Classical poets appear in Ransmayr and Nooteboom and Kadare. They also appear in *Obabakoak*, whose strikingly original form I do not have space to describe at length. Atxaga's tale is about the search for, the construction more or less *ex nihilo* of, a Basque literature which does not exist, and includes a meeting with a great Basque poet which deliberately parodies, indeed plagiarises, Dante's meeting with Virgil. The book contains tales of Obaba, a Basque town – marvellous tales, fairy tales, human stories, anecdotes – and it contains also a convention of tale-tellers who decide to plagiarise for Basque literature what it does not have, telling the bare bones of stories by Maupassant and Chekhov, García Márquez and Hemingway, Joyce and Kipling, recombined and remade as part of this eclectic work. There is a brilliantly comic and profound defence of plagiarism and set of instructions for how to rework other people's stories. The novel could almost be said to record the metamorphosis of authored stories into the plain, negotiable coin of the fund of generally available motifs and anecdotes. The narrator, obsessed with finding 'the last word' ends wordless, his brain eaten away by a lizard, which in his language is a synonym for an obsession.

This very sophisticated literary use of the tale-telling device is analogous to Calvino's brilliant *If on a Winter's Night a Traveller*, which is, in itself, what the writer in the book says he desires to write, a novel that is a series of 'Incipits' – as Nooteboom's *The Following Story* was a series of endings. *If on a Winter's Night* is and is not like Enzensberger's topological dog story. Calvino's narrator-reader is continually caught up in a hopeless search for completed versions of books whose beginnings he becomes imaginatively involved in, only to find that the rest is missing, and the offered replacement is only the beginning of a completely different tale. This brilliant meditation on, and teasing exploration of, the relations of reader and writer, is like *Obabakoak* a series of parodies of genres, styles and subjects, all of which are part of the same tapestry.

In Chapter Eight of *If on a Winter's Night* Calvino's imaginary novelist, Silas Flannery, reflects on writing. He copies out the beginning of *Crime and Punishment* to study the narrative expectation with which it is charged – 'the promise of a time of reading that extends before us and can comprise all possible developments'. He is staring at a poster of Snoopy typing 'It was a dark and stormy night'. He comments

> I would like to be able to write a book that is only an *incipit*, that maintains for its whole duration the potentiality of the beginning, the expectation still not focussed on an object. But how could such a book be constructed? Would it break off after the first paragraph? Would the preliminaries be prolonged indefinitely? Would it set the beginning of one tale inside another, as in the *Arabian Nights*?[24]

This novelist-in-a-novel is of course talking about the novel he is in. He meets a sinister and conspiratorial person called Ermes Marana, who claims to be his translator, and tells him that unauthorised translations of his books are being published in Japan. Marana is interested in fakes and replications of writings and likes Flannery because he 'could incarnate for him the ideal author, that is, the author who is dissolved in the cloud of fictions that covers the world with its thick sheath'. Flannery reflects that his own inordinate ambition has 'two paths open: either write a book that could be the unique book, that exhausts the whole in its pages; or write all books, exhaust the whole through its partial images'. These ideas lead to Proust's desire to write a collection of death-defying stories on the one hand, to rival the *Arabian Nights*, and on the other to Atxaga's idea of plagiarism, and Borges's Pierre Menard, author of the Quixote.

I was interested in the name of the faker and translator. Ermes is easy – he is Hermes the trickster, psychopomp and interpreter of riddles, lord of hermeneutics. Marana is the Spanish word for network, or fishing-net. In his preface to his *Italian Tales* Calvino uses this image of their nature.

> Ero stato, in maniere imprevista, cattaturo dalla natura tentacolare, aracnoidea, dell'oggetto del mio studio; e non era questo un modo formale ed esterno di possesso: anzi mi poneva di fronte alla sua proprieta piu segreta: la sua infinita varieta ed infinita repetizione.[25]

To call the infinity of the repetitions of the stories, in the same sentence, tentacles and spider-web is to suggest that the tales are traps, the endless labyrinths closed. Tzvetan Todorov, in his *Introduction à la littérature fantasque*[26] remarks on what he calls the '*pan-déterminisme*' of fantasy and fairy tale – touch the wand and the candle lights, throw the ring in the water and the flood stops – psychic and physical worlds are connected and causes in one have results in the other. The membrane between the two is permeable.

'Fairy tales are closed systems, that is what makes them so terrifying.' This is a quotation from Cees Nooteboom's *In the Dutch Mountains* which enacts an extraordinary questioning of the way myth and story work in our lives. I was once asked to write the 'fairy story of my life' for a collection, and wrote one called 'The Eldest Princess' about an eldest daughter who goes on a quest where she knows she must fail because she is the eldest, so steps off the path into the wild forest, and makes her own trackless future (avoiding handsome woodcutters, as well). Nooteboom's Dutch Mountains are an imaginary Dutch South where everything is the opposite of Dutch flatness and empiricism. His story is about a perfect pair of lovers, Kai and Lucia, conjurers who go south. Kai is captured by an icy woman who keeps him imprisoned in snow and mirrors; Lucia lives with a warm woman and a sunny millenarian anarchist. Nooteboom's narrator and alter ego is a Spanish Road Inspector from Zaragoza, (possibly no accident, given Potocki) and the opening of the story combines journey with death. About halfway along route C221 Tiburon says, is a cemetery.

> There is something irrevocable about it: you, as a traveller, have no choice but to accept it, this patch is reserved for death.
>
> Something similar, I think, also happens to the reader. A book is a document and into this document the word *death* is suddenly introduced, though you can, of course, have any thoughts you like about that.[27]

Part of Nooteboom's interest in this book is to distinguish between myth and fairy tale. He has an ambivalent relationship with his own upbringing as a Catholic, and at one point describes a riddling encounter between his narrator and a Flemish woman hitchhiker who meet at a monastery. The Dutchwoman describes Christianity, with contempt, as a 'fairy tale'. The Spaniard thinks that Christianity was not included in Robert Graves's Larousse encyclopaedia of mythology because Christian believers still existed, and reflects that myths have no authors, they just happen, whilst fairy tales are written down by someone. The Grimms and Calvino would disagree with this, but Nooteboom's narrator is at odds with that coercive (and sentimentally Christian) literary fairy-story creator, Hans Andersen.

> Myths were not written by anyone – it must have something
> to do with that. The writing of fairy tales is a false longing for
> the writing of myths, and therefore a longing to be no one, or
> to be a whole people, a mass without name or face, a vanished
> species. But it was too late for that.

Nooteboom's version of the closeness of humans and creatures in the world of the fairy tale is also couched as a criticism of its pan-determinism. In fairy tales, he says, people and animals 'are of equal value . . . They can move only in one direction, and reflection is therefore useless.' He reflects that in Andersen's tales inanimate objects too – important candles, ambitious rockets – have the life of determined narrative. He writes elegantly of Kundera's and Plato's ideas of erotic love, and compares a Spanish writer Eugenio d'Ors.

> Kundera and d'Ors wrote novels. Plato wrote down a myth
> that Aristophanes had told during the symposium. Andersen
> wrote fairy tales. Novels describe how life is because it *can* be
> so. In a myth an impossible answer is given to unanswerable
> questions. Something happens there that never happens
> anywhere. Myths are examples, novels are pictures, fairy tales
> are beloved lies told by people who find the failed myth of life
> intolerable. In myths people live forever. In fairy tales they live
> happily ever after. In novels there is, at the end of the 'ever
> after', the beginning of unhappiness, and usually even before.
>   In myths everything is solved in some way or other; in
> novels nothing is ever solved; and in fairy tales the solution is
> postponed, but if it ever takes place it will be outside the scope
> of the fairy tale. That is the lie.

I said earlier that storytelling was to do with death and biological time, with our own beginnings, middles and ends. I said also that stories, and story-webs, often carry within themselves images of infinity which contradict the linear narrative. There is a particular group of images of infinity, besides tentacles and spider-webs, that suggest a *bad infinity*, a trap. These are mirrors, which go with one aspect of death. Nooteboom describes his Kai trapped in a room of mirrors in the snowy mountains. Before him, Andersen's Kai was susceptible to the Snow Queen because a splinter of an enchanted mirror had pierced his heart. In *The Following Story* Nooteboom's Socrates after making love to his biologist says that he suddenly saw himself as

> a man alone in a cube, surrounded by invisible others in adjacent cubes, and with tens of thousands of pages around me filled with descriptions of the same, but ever distinct, emotions of real or invented persons.

This is the similarity, and endless difference of love. But when dead Socrates goes back to a restaurant with 'a thousand mirrors in a cabinet encrusted with gold . . . reflected in a forest of mirrors . . . with, further and further away the lights of chandeliers sparkling in my thousand bespectacled eyes' he reflects

> Mirrors are useless. They retain nothing, not the living and not the dead, they are mercenary perjurers, nauseating in their glassy deference.

Atxaga has a splendid variant on the Appointment at Samarra, in which the servant fleeing the appointment with death is offered a refuge by a cunning friend in a shop where Death will not find him. At dawn a black figure is seen leaving the store of the mirror-maker, carrying a mirror. Mirrors create a false infinity and defeat death.

One of the best stories I know about the dangerous aspect of the network of tales is by Terry Pratchett who writes wise and comic fantasies set in the Discworld. In this one three witches set out to stop a Princess from marrying a transfigured frog in a city called Genua which is in the power of a witch called Lilith, who works magic with mirrors to make everyone's lives conform to a fairy-story vision of the world, and fairy-story expectations of satisfactory plots, intrigues and endings. (Pratchett is very good on the misery of animal minds trapped in human metamorphoses. His wolves, snakes, frogs and even cats are anguished and distorted.) Pratchett in my view is one of the great modern storytellers. Here is his introduction of the idea of stories.

> People think stories are shaped by people. In fact, it's the other way round.
>
> Stories can exist independently of their players. If you know that, the knowledge is power.
>
> Stories, great flapping ribbons of shaped space-time, have been blowing and uncoiling around the universe since the beginning of time. And they have evolved. The weakest have died and the strongest have survived and they have grown fat on the retelling . . .
>
> And their very existence overlays a faint but insistent pattern on the chaos that is history. Stories etch grooves deep enough for people to follow in the same way that water follows certain paths down a mountainside. And every time fresh actors tread the path of the story the groove runs deeper.
>
> This is called the theory of narrative causality and it means that a story, once started, *takes a shape*. It picks up all the vibrations of all the other workings of that story that have ever been.
>
> That is why history keeps on repeating all the time.
>
> So a thousand heroes have stolen fire from the gods. A thousand wolves have eaten grandmother, a thousand princesses have been kissed . . .
>
> Stories don't care who takes part in them. All that matters is that the story gets told, that the story repeats. Or, if you prefer to think of it like this: stories are a parasitical life form, warping lives in the service only of the story itself.[28]

Compare Nooteboom, 'The fairy tale is a fungus on reality. Travesty, apology, fungus, disease, caricature.' (*In the Dutch Mountains*)

In Pratchett's tale, the good witches proceed across the discworld undoing stories that are waiting to happen, waking sleeping beauties, saving wolves from being grandmothers, returning the frog to his pool and diet of flies. Lilith, or Lily Weatherwax, in her fairy-tale castle not unlike Oz, has a cabinet of mirrors which is shattered by her disreputable sister. She is then trapped in the mirrors, where she has a revealing conversation with Death, one of Pratchett's most endearing characters, who is a skeleton with a scythe because that is what is expected, and speaks in small capital letters.

> Lily Weatherwax looked out at the multi-layered silvery world.
> 'Where am I?'
> INSIDE THE MIRROR.
> 'Am I dead?'
> THE ANSWER TO THAT, said Death, IS SOMEWHERE BETWEEN NO AND YES.
> Lily turned, and a billion figures turned with her.
> 'When can I get out?'
> WHEN YOU FIND THE ONE THAT'S REAL.
> Lily Weatherwax ran on through the endless reflections.

Death makes stories real, and false infinities mean that death is not death, but 'somewhere between no and yes', as he says.

There is an interesting discussion, in Robert Irwin's excellent *Companion to the Arabian Nights*, of the kind of Fate which operates in such tales, so that each character 'has his fate written on his forehead'. Harun al Raschid may dismiss his vizier because of something he's read, and the vizier, returning after many adventures may find them already written in Harun's book. Fate is a character in such tales, Irwin tells us, and free will and destiny are only aspects of each other. But he goes on to discuss Pasolini's description of the 'disappearance of destiny' at the end of each tale, as it is replaced by 'the somnolence of daily life'. He then quotes Benjamin's essay on 'Fate and Characters' where Benjamin remarks that misfortune is a category of fate, but that 'happiness is rather, what releases man from the embroilment of the Fates and from the net of his own fate'. 'Happy ever after' is, as Nooteboom said, a lie, a look in a mirror. Ordinary happiness is to be outside a story, full of curiosity, looking before and after.

· 6 ·

Ice, Snow, Glass

One of the surprising things about glass, to northerners, must have been its resemblance to ice, and its difference from ice. Glass is made from sand, heated and melted; ice is a form of water, which shifts from solid to liquid with the seasons. The fairy stories which I now see provided much of my secret imagery as a child are northern tales about ice, glass, and mirrors. It is surprising how often they go together. Hans Andersen's *The Snow Queen* opens with the splintering of a great mirror. *Snow White* has a heroine named for the whiteness of snow, a wicked stepmother entranced by a speaking mirror, and a glass coffin melted, so to speak, by a kiss. Then there is the Norwegian story, a version of the Atalanta myth, in which the unattainable princess sits at the top of a glass mountain, throwing down golden apples to the suitors who try to mount it. As a child I used to think of that great transparent spike indifferently as glass and ice, cold, hard, glittering. When I was grown-up I found the story of the *Glass Coffin* in the Brothers Grimm, and rewrote it into *Possession*. I shall start by looking at these tales, and then look at the sometimes paradoxical and private uses I made of them.

The Grimms' *Snow White* opens with falling snow. 'It was once midwinter, and the snowflakes fell like feathers from the sky, and there sat a queen by a window, that had a frame of ebony, and she sewed. And whilst she sewed, and looked out at the snow, she pricked herself in the finger with the needle, and three drops of blood fell in the snow. And because the red looked so beautiful in the white snow, she thought to herself, 'If I were to have a child, white as snow, red as blood, and black as the ebony frame . . .'[1] Snow White is born and the queen dies in the same moment. The king marries again, and the first thing we are told about the stepmother is that she is proud and beautiful and has a magic mirror that speaks the truth, and tells her that she is the fairest in the land. The story takes its way; Snow White grows to be the fairest; the stepmother orders her death; she lives with the dwarves, and is visited by the wicked queen, who tries to kill her with a coloured lace, with a poisoned comb, and finally with a poisoned apple, 'white with rosy cheeks', which causes her to fall down 'dead'. When the dwarves find her lying there, they cannot bury her 'in the black earth' because she 'still looks as fresh as a living person, and has still her beautiful red cheeks'. So they make a transparent glass coffin, in which she lies 'a long long time' still 'as white as snow, as red as blood, and black-haired as ebony-wood'. The prince comes, says he cannot live out of her sight, carries away the coffin, and dislodges the poisoned apple, so that Snow White is restored to life, and becomes his wife. And the wicked queen's mirror tells her the young queen is a thousand times more beautiful, and she is made to dance herself to death in 'red-glowing' heated iron shoes.

Even as a child I was entranced by the patterning of this, the weaving of the three colours, the framing in glass of faces and stages of lives. Andersen's tale is a literary work, and has, as Keats said of didactic poetry, designs on the reader. It comes out of the complex of stories about Snow White and Rose Red, and changes the imagery, adding a kind of personal terror to the elemental one. It opens, as readers do not always remember, with a wicked, mocking magician, who has invented a mirror which shrinks the good and beautiful, and magnifies the ugly and useless, making the loveliest landscapes look like boiled spinach. This mirror is carried into the sky by his magical pupils, dropped to earth and smashed into millions of fragments, which get into people's eyes, or are made into windows and spectacles, distorting everything to the 'perverted and corrupted'. 'Some people were so unfortunate as to receive a little splinter into their hearts – that was terrible! the heart became cold and hard like a lump of ice.'[2]

The two children in the story, Kay and Gerda, tend beautiful rose-trees on their roofs, and are happy until the arrival of the Snow Queen, who is queen of the 'white bees', the snowflakes, and who 'breathes with her frosty breath on the windows, and then they are covered with strange and beautiful forms, like trees and flowers'. Kay sees the Snow Queen, who does not harm him – 'there was a clear frost next day, and soon afterwards came spring – the trees and flowers budded, the swallows built their nest, the windows were opened . . . the roses blossomed beautifully that summer.' But then Kay gets a splinter of the mirror in his eye and in his heart. He destroys the roses, tears up books of fairy tales, mocks Gerda, and becomes entranced by the mathematical beauty of the snowflakes seen through a 'burning glass'. The Snow Queen reappears, Kay attaches his sled to hers and is carried away. 'A more intelligent, more lovely countenance he could not imagine; she no longer appeared to him ice, cold ice . . .' They fly off into the raging storm, and Kay becomes obsessed with the beauty of maths, and statistics, and puzzles.

Gerda, meanwhile, sets out to find him, and is entrapped by a kindly witch who has a lovely garden, and a cottage with high windows 'with panes of different coloured glass, red, blue and yellow, so that when the bright daylight streamed through them, various and beautiful were the hues reflected upon the room'. She lives in a rosy enchantment, with cherries to eat and crimson silk cushions, but the witch waves her crutch and causes the roses to sink underground, in case they remind Gerda of her quest for Kay. Gerda's tears, however, when she sees the rose painted on the old lady's hat, cause the roses to spring up and talk to her – they tell her Kay is not dead and underground, for they have been there, so she sets off again, on a series of comic adventures, and finally, aided by a raven, a robber-maiden, a Lapland Woman and a Finland Woman, and a reindeer, finds Kay in the Snow Queen's palace, after a very Victorian combat between an army of living snowflakes 'like snakes rolled into knots, like great ugly porcupines, like little fat bears with bristling hair' and an army of 'little bright angels' formed from the vapour of Gerda's breath as she prays. Kay is piecing together a jigsaw made of the fragments of a shattered frozen lake, which Andersen calls 'the ice-puzzle of reason'. He cannot form the word 'Eternity', but when Gerda sings a hymn about the Infant Jesus, the word forms itself, and the children are able to escape back to the world of roses and summer. It seems significant that it is not the crucified God, but the Christ-child who initiates Kay and Gerda into the human perpetuity of birth after death – the earthly version of eternity, spring and rebirth, not the cold mathematical one.

The story of the princess on the glass mountain needs less elaboration – it is one of those about the third son, the Ash-Lad, who acquires three magic horses and suits of armour, and rides up to the contest, each day more glorious than the one before, and confounds the assembled suitors, including his lazy brothers. The princess sits on 'a high high hill, all of glass, as smooth and slippery as ice', with three gold apples in her lap, and watches her suitors. When she sees the Ash-Lad, she wants him to win, and throws the apples after him, one at each attempt. He reveals himself, much like the ash-girl, Cinderella, who reveals that she has the glass slipper in her possession, and when the king sees his golden mail under his sooty rags he says he well deserves the princess and half the kingdom.[3]

The Grimms' *The Glass Coffin* is about an indomitable Little Tailor who discovers in an underground fastness not one but two glass cases, one containing a miniature palace with stables and outhouses 'carefully and elegantly worked' and the other a beautiful maiden with long golden hair, wrapped in a rich cloak. He releases the maiden, who gives him 'a friendly kiss on his mouth', calls him her heaven-sent husband, and tells him how she was imprisoned by a magician, a 'Schwarzkunstler' or 'Black-artist' who had turned her brother into a stag, and her servants into blue smoke imprisoned in glass flasks. After the rescue, the stag is turned back into a man, and the tailor and the lady are married.[4]

There are obvious symbolic oppositions in all these stories, which I'll discuss first. Red and white, ice and fire, snow and blood, life and death. In all the stories the frozen sleep, or death-in-life, of the ice-princess is a kind of isolation, a separate virginal state, from which she is released by the kiss, the opener, the knight on horseback. The combination of needle, blood, and snow at the beginning of *Snow White* resembles the prick of the fairy spindle which begins the long sleep of *Sleeping Beauty*, amongst her hedge of roses and thorns, through which the prince breaks his way to wake her with a kiss. Snow White's mother bleeds, bears her desired daughter, and dies, and her daughter is red, white and black. The princess on the glass hill is isolated in her pride and her beauty, put at a distance by coldness and glitter, with golden apples in her lap. She throws down the apples to the handsome young man, and descends from the mountain. In Andersen's story, it is Gerda, the female child, who is in touch with warmth, flowering roses, cherries, and the human heart. The cold woman takes the young man away into her ice palace where she keeps him from the ordinary cycle of life and affection. Gerda rescues him for redness and warmth and the seasons. The ice palace is a false eternity, a duration outside time, to be escaped from. The lady in the glass coffin was bewitched because she hoped to have eternal happiness without marriage, communing with her beloved brother in their happy castle. The Black-artist's spell put her into a sleep resembling the sleep of Snow White and Sleeping Beauty, which Bettelheim has said may be a figure of the drowsiness and lethargy of girls at puberty; she is rescued by a husband, not a brother, to whom she offers the kiss of life.

But that wasn't how it felt to me as a girl, or not entirely, although I would probably have been able to explain the conventional 'meaning' of the kiss, the awakening out of ice, the marriage and living happy ever after. I think I knew, even then, that there was something secretly good, illicitly desirable, about the ice-hills and glass barriers. Snow White's mother died, and no one appears to have minded. It was natural. She was a woman, living a normal woman's fate. There was something wonderful about being beautiful and shining and high up with a lap full of golden fruit, something which was lost with human love, with the descent to be kissed and given away. Hans Andersen's Snow Queen was not only beautiful but intelligent and powerful; she gave Kay a vision of beauty and order, from which Gerda, with Andersen's blessing, redeemed him for the ordinary and the everyday. Andersen makes a standard opposition between cold reason and warm-heartedness and comes down whole-heartedly on the side of warm-heartedness, adding to it his own insistent Christian message. The eternity of the beautiful snow-crystals is a false infinity; only Gerda's invocation of the Infant Jesus allows a glimpse of true eternity. Andersen even cheats by making the beautiful, mathematically perfect snowflakes into nasty gnomes and demons, snakes, hedgehogs, bears, the things that torment the lazy daughter in the story of Mother Holle who makes snow by shaking out her feather-bed. Science and reason are bad, kindness is good. It is a frequent, but not a necessary opposition. And I found in it, and in the dangerous isolation of the girl on her slippery shiny height a figure of what was beginning to bother me, the conflict between a female destiny, the kiss, the marriage, the child-bearing, the death, and the frightening loneliness of cleverness, the cold distance of seeing the world through art, of putting a frame round things.

All these stories have images of art, as well as of defloration and life-and-death. The queen in *Snow White* is entranced by a black frame round a window, making a beautiful image with red and white, warm blood and cold snow. Snow White herself is the creation of an aesthetic perception, and she becomes an object of aesthetic perception, framed in her glass coffin, so beautiful that the Prince wants to carry the case everywhere.* The wicked stepmother is also obsessed with beauty, of course – her own beauty, contemplated in the self-referring gaze of the mirror. There appears to be no glass between the first queen's ebony frame and the snow on to which she bleeds – she lives without glass between her and the world, and she dies as a result. The wicked queen burns because her only relationship is with the mirror. Snow White is possibly the middle term – alive, preserved intact by the transparent barrier between her and the world. It is the wicked wizard's mirror that has entered Kay's heart, making him cold, but the Snow Queen has a truth, an interest that Andersen is afraid of, which is not self-reflecting. Even as a little girl I could not see why the beauty of the snowflakes should be bad, or what was wrong with reason. Graham Greene wrote that every artist has a splinter of ice in his heart, and I think artists recognise the distancing of glass and ice as an ambivalent matter, both chilling and life-giving, saving as well as threatening. When as a grown woman I first read *The Glass Coffin* I was entranced by the images of artistry the storyteller used to describe the miniature castle in the glass case, the craftsmanship the tailor sees in

* Our perception of Snow White's beauty is inevitably conditioned by Disney's doll-like heroine. Alison Lurie once made the point that it is impossible for American children not to see fairy-tale people in Disney's forms, whereas the European child, at least until recently, had a chance of imagining real beauty, dangerous perfect loveliness. Disney's wicked queen has a lot of furious energy, and the mirror has a demonic power, but Snow White herself is anodyne and squeaking, and the kitsch animals don't help with the bridge from fairy tale into myth.

what is in fact a product of the Black Arts, a reduction of Life to Life-in-Death. A fabricated world in a glass case gives a delight an ordinary castle doesn't. When I rewrote the story in *Possession* I made the tailor kill the Black-artist with an ice-splinter that is not in Grimm, and I made him regret his own art, when married to his rich lady. The story in *Possession* is told by Christabel LaMotte, woman and artist, who is deeply afraid that any ordinary human happiness may be purchased at the expense of her art, that maybe she needs to be alone in her golden hair on her glass eminence, an ice-maiden.

A tale I always associated with the ice and glass was Tennyson's 'Lady of Shalott'; I must have known it by heart as a small girl, since we had a colouring book with the poem and pages of pre-Raphaelite images to colour in. The Lady has things in common with the frozen death-in-life states of Snow White and of the lady and her castle in the glass coffins. She is enclosed in her tower, and sees the world not even through the window, but in a mirror, which reflects the outside life, which she, the artist, then weaves into 'a magic web with colours gay'. She is not the Wicked Queen; she does not reflect herself. She is 'half-sick of shadows', which as a girl I always took to be a reflection of the sense that the life of books was more real and brighter than the everyday, but ought not to be. (There are other possible interpretations which I shan't go into on this occasion.) When the colour of the outside life is specified (apart from the blue of the sky) it is red – the 'red cloaks of market girls', or 'long-haired page in crimson clad'. Sir Lancelot is shining and flaming; he is a red-cross knight, whose 'helmet and the helmet-feather/Burn'd like one burning flame together,' and he has coal-black curls. This mixture of sun and flame causes the Lady to leave her enclosed space, to look out of the window-frame, which causes the mirror to crack from side to side, and the magic web to float wide. Once the Lady embarks on her last voyage she takes on the images of ice and glass.

> And down the river's dim expanse
> Like some bold seer in a trance
> Seeing all his own mischance –
> With a glassy countenance
> Did she look to Camelot.

She lies 'robed in snowy white', and sings

> Till her blood was frozen slowly
> And her eyes were darken'd wholly . . .
> A gleaming shape she floated by
> Dead-pale between the houses high . . .

The Lady was solitary and alive, even if the magic colours bright were only shadows and reflections. Once she steps out towards flesh and blood she suffers part of the fate of Snow White's mother who looked out, and desired a child. Her floating catafalque has a feeling of a glass coffin, and the illustrations of my childhood book corresponded to that feeling.

Preserving solitude and distance, staying cold and frozen, may, for women as well as artists, be a way of preserving life. A correlated figure who fascinated me and found her way into my work was Elizabeth I, the Virgin Queen, whose ambivalent image runs through *The Virgin in the Garden*. Elizabeth preserved her power in the world by not bleeding in any sense – she preserved her virginity, and was not beheaded, like her mother and her great rival, Mary Queen of Scots, both of whom came down the ice mountain and tried to be passionate and powerful simultaneously. A poem written about her:

> Under a tree I saw a Virgin sit
> The red and white rose quartered in her face . . .

was ostensibly about her combination of York and Lancaster in the Tudor Rose, but I read it as a combination of Snow White and Rose Red in one self-sufficient person. She wrote a love-lyric, I read, when turning away her suitors:

> I am and am not, I freeze and yet am burned,
> Since from my selfe another selfe I turned.[5]

She was unchanging, *semper eadem* as her motto said, a kind of Snow Queen. She made the opposite choice from Snow White's mother and the Lady of Shalott. And she wrote wonderful prose, and good poems;

she was clever, and self-determined.

John Beer, in his interesting essay, 'Ice and Spring' on Coleridge's imaginative education,[6] points out that ice in Coleridge's early thought was associated conventionally with 'the icy dart of death' but that later he came to be more riddling and ambivalent about it, to be interested in the possibilities of preserving living things by freezing them, in ice as one extreme of the forms of the universe, so that frost at midnight is a 'secret ministry' making beautiful forms of the 'silent icicles/Quietly shining to the quiet Moon'.

The Ancient Mariner is becalmed on a hot slimy sea under a bloody sun, but the Albatross, the benevolent creature from the land of ice and snow, was sent by a good spirit, who 'loved the bird that loved the man, Who shot him with his bow'. Kubla Khan builds a 'miracle of rare device/A sunny pleasure-dome with caves of ice' and Coleridge is happier with the balance between the inanimate beauty of ice, crystalline forms, and warm organic ones than, as we have seen, Hans Andersen. Ice and snow are part of the cycle of the seasons, and life-forms frozen and dormant are also preserved in the cold. Neither Kay, nor Snow White are dead; they are part of a vegetation myth, waiting for the spring. In this sense they are associated with another ambiguous figure, the Queen Hermione of *The Winter's Tale* who does and does not die when her daughter is born. She is said to be dead, but at the miraculous ending, she is restored in the form of a stone statue that has been kept hidden in a vault. I always see this statue as white marble, although it cannot be, and is described as painted. It is a dead woman preserved as a work of art, who then turns out to be a living woman. The connections of living blood and cold stone as Leontes looks at the 'statue' are disturbing.

Leontes	Would you not deem it breath'd? and that those veins
	Did verily bear blood?
Polixenes	Masterly done
	The very life seems warm upon her lip.
Leontes	The fixure of her eye has motion in't,
	As we are mock'd with art.[7]

And later, when Leontes tries to kiss the statue, to bring it to life with the kiss, in terms of the myth, he is warned off because the redness is only artfulness, paint.

> Paulina   Good my lord, forbear:
> The ruddiness upon her lips is wet;
> You'll mar it if you kiss it, stain your own
> With oily painting.

It is Hermione's son, Mamillius, who says 'A sad tale's best for winter', and it is Mamillius who dies of grief when Hermione 'dies' in giving birth to her daughter, the Perdita who makes the spring flower speech about the pale primroses that die unmarried (amongst others) invoking the flowers that Proserpina let fall when 'gloomy Dis' was about to bear her away to his dark kingdom. Perdita is part of a consoling myth of renaissance and rebirth; Mamillius dies a real, final death of grief; Hermione is a riddle, a woman who has preserved herself by keeping herself apart from her life and its threats, though this has entailed the loss of one, possibly two, children. In my private iconography, which is of course very public, for myths have their life from general belief, Hermione's ruddy lips and stony figure are associated with the dead whiteness and red lips of the portraits of Elizabeth I, and with that most powerful of white faces, Keats's Moneta in *The Fall of Hyperion*. Moneta is a figure for Mnemosyne, or memory.

> Then saw I a wan face,
> Not pined by human sorrows, but bright-blanched
> By an immortal sickness which kills not;
> It works a constant change, which happy death
> Can put no end to; deathwards progressing
> To no death was that visage; it had passed
> The lily and the snow; and beyond these
> I must not think now, though I saw that face –
> But for her eyes I should have fled away.

Moneta is 'visionless entire' 'of all external things', and speaks to the artist in the poet – she has something in common with the Lady of Shalott, though she is more extreme. She is preserved again in a duration outside everyday time, like the Snow Queen; her sickness is also a strength and a wisdom.

Another pair of women I associate with the wisdom of the stories of Snow White and the Snow Queen are Dorothea and Rosamond in *Middlemarch*. There is a sense in which this pair of marriageable virgins, at the beginning of the story, are Snow White and Rose Red. Dorothea is white, has a nun-like quality, and is compared (ironically) to the Blessed Virgin in the second sentence of Chapter 1. She is also clever, interested in ideas and ideals, and will be interested in art. Rosamond's name itself is rose-red, Rosa Mundi, the rose of the world, another way of referring to the Virgin, of course. In one of the scenes in which readers best, ironically, remember Dorothea, she is seen on her return from her Roman wedding journey, imprisoned in her husband's house, Lowick Manor, in January. She looks out of the window. It is white and snowy. I give a long quotation because of the delicate way in which George Eliot has woven together the contrasts of red and white, fire and ice, blood and snow.

A light snow was falling as they descended at the door, and in the morning, when Dorothea passed from her dressing-room into the blue-green boudoir that we know of, she saw the long avenue of limes lifting their trunks from a white earth, and spreading white branches against the dun and motionless sky. The distant flat shrank in uniform whiteness and low-hanging uniformity of cloud. The very furniture in the room seemed to have shrunk since she saw it before: the stag in the tapestry looked more like a ghost in his ghostly blue-green world; the volumes of polite literature in the bookcase looked more like immovable imitations of books. The bright fire of dry oak-boughs burning on the dogs seemed an incongruous renewal of life and glow – like the figure of Dorothea herself as she entered carrying the red-leather cases containing the cameos for Celia.

She was glowing from her morning toilette as only healthful youth can glow; there was gem-like brightness on her coiled hair and in her hazel eyes; there was warm red life in her lips; her throat had a breathing whiteness above the differing white of the fur which itself seemed to wind about her neck and cling down her blue-grey pelisse with a tenderness gathered from her own, a sentient commingled innocence which kept its loveliness against the crystalline purity of the out-door snow. (*Middlemarch*, Chapter 28)

Rosamond is called Rosy, by her husband and family; in Chapter 46, as one example, she appears in 'her cherry-coloured dress with swansdown trimming about the throat'. But her rosiness is not warmth; she is a parody of the domestic comfort of Gerda's homemaking. The fairytale image most often applied to Rosamond, I imagine, is that of the water-nixie, or melusine, or Lorelei, a cold-blooded fairy who entangles men to drown them, and has no soul. But in terms of the Snow White tales, she is not Rose Red but the wicked queen, and the opening of Chapter 27, which precedes the chapter in which Dorothea stares out of the window at the snow, Rosamond is associated with one of the most striking mirror-images in literature, which again I'll quote in full.

> An eminent philosopher among my friends, who can dignify even your ugly furniture by lifting it into the serene light of science, has shown me this pregnant little fact. Your pier-glass or extensive surface of polished steel made to be rubbed by a housemaid, will be minutely and multitudinously scratched in all directions; but place now against it a lighted candle as a centre of illumination, and lo! the scratches will seem to arrange themselves in a fine series of concentric circles round that little sun. It is demonstrable that the scratches are going everywhere impartially, and it is only your candle which produces the flattering illusion of a concentric arrangement, its light falling with an exclusive optical selection. These things are a parable. The scratches are events, and the candle is the egoism of any person now absent – of Miss Vincy, for example. Rosamond had a Providence of her own who had kindly made her more charming than other girls . . .

Rosamond is outwardly rosy and inwardly glassy; Dorothea is outwardly pale, but inwardly 'ardent' or burning. My friend, the psychoanalyst

Ignês Sodré, has written about a later moment when Dorothea, still trapped and now widowed, looks out of a window after a sleepless night of decision, and sees 'a man with a bundle on his back and a woman carrying her baby' and feels the desire to join 'that involuntary palpitating life' and no longer to be a spectator. As a result of this, she is able to approach Will Ladislaw, break the grip of her husband's dead hand, and have everyday human happiness after all, the kiss of the prince, the husband, the child. George Eliot's last words about her heroine are ambivalent. 'Certainly those determining acts of her life were not ideally beautiful . . .' 'Her finely-touched spirit still had its fine issues, though they were not widely visible.' She was, we are to believe, happy and good, and alive, and that is much. But her creator chose differently, though she also was ardent and passionate, and did not keep herself to herself. There is a wonderful contrast of red and white, when Dorothea, on her unhappy honeymoon journey in Rome, is overwhelmed by the power of the layers of ancient life and thought. She is a provincial innocent, 'fed on meagre Protestant histories and on art chiefly of the hand-screen sort'. (You can *hear* the curl of George Eliot's lip.) What she sees is white and bloodless.

> Ruins and basilicas, palaces and colossi, set in the midst of a sordid present, where all that was living and warm-blooded seemed sunk in the deep degeneracy of a superstition divorced from reverence; the dimmer but yet eager Titanic life gazing and struggling on walls and ceilings; the long vistas of white forms whose marble eyes seemed to hold the monotonous light of an alien world . . . Forms both pale and glowing took possession of her young sense, and fixed themselves in her memory even when she was not thinking of them, preparing strange associations which remained through her after-years.

And Dorothea sees this alien, monotonous whiteness through a threatening veil of red, the 'red drapery' which in St Peter's 'was being hung for Christmas spreading itself everywhere like a disease of the retina'. George Eliot, in her need to employ the red colour, got the season wrong – the red drapery is for the Passion and resurrection at Easter. And the power of the writing is evidence that George Eliot, unlike her heroine, was shocked into excitement, into a desire to know, even into emulation, by the contrast between art of the hand-screen sort and the power of European culture and history.

I always, for myself, associate Eliot's 'white forms whose marble eyes hold the monotonous light of an alien world' with Keats's Moneta, who distinguishes between artists and dreamers. I also associate them with the more beautiful frozen white forms on Keats's ambiguous Grecian urn, those marble men and maidens who will love forever and never kiss, under dark eternal forest boughs, on a work of art which remains perpetually virginal, a 'still unravished bride of quietness', a 'silent form' which

> dost tease us out of thought
> As doth eternity: Cold Pastoral!
> When old age shall this generation waste,
> Thou shalt remain, in midst of other woe
> Than ours . . .

The child I was found an illicit encouragement (which was also a warning of coldness) under the ostensible message of the ice-tales. When I was an undergraduate I used to puzzle over W.B.Yeats's dictum

> A man must choose
> Perfection of the life, or of the work,
> And if he choose the latter, must reject
> A heavenly mansion, raging in the dark . . .

The frozen, stony women became my images of choosing the perfection of the work, rejecting (so it seemed to me then, though I have done my best to keep my apple and swallow it) the imposed biological cycle, blood, kiss, roses, birth, death, and the hungry generations. These stories are riddles, and all readers change them a little, and they accept and resist change simultaneously.

· 7 ·

The Greatest Story Ever Told

The greatest story ever told? Perhaps the story of the two brothers, both kings, who found that their wives were unfaithful, took bloody vengeance, and set out into the world to travel until and unless they found someone less fortunate than themselves. They encountered a demon with a woman in a glass chest with four locks; she came out whilst he slept and insisted on sex with the princes. She collected their rings to make a round hundred from such chance lovers. The princes decided that the demon was more unfortunate than they were and returned to their kingdoms. There the elder brother, Shahriyar, instituted a reign of terror, marrying a virgin each day, and handing her to his vizier for execution at dawn. The vizier's daughter Shahrazad, a woman both wise and learned, requested her father to give her to the king. On the wedding night, the bride asked that her younger sister, Dinarzad, might sleep under the bed, and when the king had 'finished with Shahrazad' the girl asked her sister to tell a story to while away the time until dawn. When dawn came the story was not finished, and the curious prince stayed execution for a night. And the characters in that story told other tales, and those too were unfinished at dawn, and before other dawns gave rise to other tales. And the prince's narrative curiosity kept the princess alive, day after day. She narrated a stay of execution, a space in which she bore three children. And in the end, the king removed the sentence of death, and they lived happily ever after.

This story has everything a tale should have. Sex, death, treachery, vengeance, magic, humour, warmth, wit, surprise and a happy ending.

It appears to be a story against women, but leads to the appearance of one of the strongest and cleverest heroines in world literature, who triumphs because she is endlessly inventive and keeps her head. The *Thousand and One Nights* are stories about storytelling – without ever ceasing to be stories about love and life and death and money and food and other human necessities. Narration is as much part of human nature as breath and the circulation of the blood. Modernist literature tried to do away with storytelling, which it thought was vulgar, replacing it with flashbacks, epiphanies, streams of consciousness. But storytelling is intrinsic to biological time, which we cannot escape. Life, Pascal once said, is like living in a prison, from which every day fellow prisoners are taken away to be executed. We are all, like Scheherazade, under sentence of death, and we all think of our lives as narratives, with beginnings, middles and ends. Storytelling in general, and the *Thousand and One Nights* in particular, consoles us for endings with endless new beginnings. I finished my condensed version of the frame story with the European fairy-tale ending, 'they lived happily ever after', which is a consolatory false eternity, for no one does, except in the endless repetitions of storytelling. Stories are like genes, they keep part of us alive after the end of our story, and there is something very moving about Scheherazade entering on the happiness ever after, not at her wedding, but after 1001 tales and three children.

Great stories, and great story-collections, are shape-shifters. The *Thousand and One Nights* first appeared in Europe in the French translation of Antoine Galland, between 1704 and 1717. He used a fourteenth-century Syrian text, but adapted and rewrote and added for French taste – it is possible that both *Aladdin* and *Ali Baba* as we read them originate with the Frenchman. The tales, according to Husain Haddawy, had been circulating in one form or another since the ninth century. They have both Persian and Indian originals – Haddawy's recent elegant translation of part of them is based on Muhsin Mahdi's definitive edition of the fourteenth-century manuscript in the Bibliothèque Nationale (*Alf Layla wa Layla*, Leiden, 1984.) Subsequent translators took liberties, or used their imaginations. Richard Burton invented a curious convoluted Victorian-mediaeval style. Joseph Charles Mardrus, in 1899, according to Robert Irwin, whose *Companion* to the Arabian Nights is gripping and indispensable, 'reshaped the *Nights* in such a manner that the stories appear to have been written by Oscar Wilde or Stéphane Mallarmé'. Eastern and Western literature contain other related collections of interlinked tales – the *Katha Sarit Sagara*, translated as *The Ocean of Story* in 1928, Ovid's *Metamorphoses*, Chaucer's *Canterbury Tales*, and Boccaccio's *Decameron*, whose frame-story has its characters defying the Black Death by retreating to the country and telling tales. A direct descendant of the *Nights* is *The Saragossa Manuscript*, written by the Polish Jean Potocki between 1797 and 1815. Potocki was a Knight of Malta, a linguist and an occultist – his tales, set in Spain in 1739, are dizzily interlinked at many levels – ghouls, politics, rationalism, ghosts, necromancy, tale within tale within tale. He spent time searching vainly for a manuscript of the *Nights* in Morocco, and shot himself with a silver bullet made from a teapot-lid in Poland. Out of such works came nineteenth-century Gothick fantasy, and the intricate, paranoid nightmare plottings of such story-webs as *The Crying of Lot 49* or Lawrence Norfolk's *Lemprière's Dictionary*. Collections of tales talk to each other and borrow from each other, motifs glide from culture to culture, century to century. If the origin of stories is the human ability to remember the past, speculate about beginnings, and imagine the ending, it doesn't follow that the search for any 'pure' or undisputed paternal or maternal origin for any story will lead to definiteness.

Scheherazade's tales have lived on, like germ-cells, in many literatures. In British Romantic poetry the Arabian Nights stood for the wonderful against the mundane, the imaginative against the prosaically and reductively rational. Coleridge said his mind had been 'habituated *to the vast*' by his early reading of 'Romances, & Relations of Giants & Magicians, & Genii'. He used the tale of the angry and vengeful Djinn whose invisible child had been killed by a thrown datestone, as an example of pure chance or fate. Wordsworth, in the fifth book of *The Prelude*, describes his childhood treasure, 'a little yellow, canvas-covered book,/A slender abstract of the Arabian tales' and the 'promise scarcely earthly' of his discovery that there were four large volumes of the work. Dreamers and forgers of lawless tales, he says, confer visionary power. Earlier in Book V he tells of a dream encounter with a strange figure on a dromedary, who seemed to be both Don Quixote and 'an Arab of the desert too' who carries a stone and a shell, which are also 'both books' – one Euclid's *Elements* and the other a prophetic poem. The Arab is saving the 'books' from 'the fleet waters of the drowning world' – the final Deluge close at hand. Wordsworth has compressed two great collections of tales in a dream-pun, an Arabian Knight, saving geometry and poetry from destruction. Again, the Tales stand against death. And Dickens, who became the master of serial narration and endless beginnings, comforted his lonely and miserable childhood with the Arabian Nights, living in their world, and learning their craft.

Various Western writers have been tempted to write the Thousand-and-second Tale, including the American, Edgar Allan Poe, and the Viennese Joseph Roth. Roth's tale of the decadent days of the Austrian Empire, the border between East and West, is full of furtive and voluptuous sex, sly analysis of the operations of authorities, substitutions of women, vanishing jewels. Poe's Scheherazade makes the mistake of telling her ageing husband about modern marvels like steam-ships, radio and telegraphs. He finds these true tales so incredible that he concludes that she has lost her touch and has her strangled after all. Poe is a combative and irreverent Yankee at the Persian court. John Barth, in his Dunyazadiad appears in person as a balding bespectacled genie who tells the nervous Scheherazade the tales she will tell because he has read them in the future and she is his heroine – thus creating another false eternity, a circular time-loop, in which storytellers hand on stories of storytellers . . .

Then there are the modern oriental fabulists, Naguib Mahfouz and Salman Rushdie, both threatened with death for storytelling. Mahfouz's *Arabian Nights and Days* is a collection of magical tales, with a political edge and a spiritual depth. His stories rework the Nights; his Shahriyar slowly learns about justice and mercy, the Angel of Death is a bric-à-brac merchant, and genies play tricks with fate. Salman Rushdie's narratives are all intertwined with the storytelling of the Nights. *Haroun and the Sea of Stories* pits a resourceful child, Haroun, against the evil Khattam-Shud who wants to drain the Ocean of the Streams of Story, which are alive, and replace it with silence and darkness. Rushdie's tale, like Scheherazade's, equates storytelling with life, but his characters and wit owe as much to western fantasies, to Alice in Wonderland and the Wizard of Oz, as they do to the ancient

Ocean of Stories or the *Thousand and One Nights*. Another cross-fertilisation, another conversation.

Rushdie's Sea of Stories is 'the biggest library in the universe'. Jorge Luis Borges, to whom libraries, labyrinths, and books were all images of infinity, wrote in *The Garden of Forking Paths* of 'that night which is at the middle of the Thousand and One Nights when Scheherazade (through a magical oversight of the copyist) begins to relate word for word the story of the Thousand and one Nights, establishing the risk of coming once again to the night when she must repeat it, and thus on to infinity'. This circular tale fascinated Italo Calvino (who failed to find the episode in any translation of the Nights). Calvino's own marvellous *If on a Winter's Night a Traveller* is the endless tale of a lost Reader who keeps beginning books only to find the rest is missing, and the replacement copy turns out to be always another, quite different beginning. This novel contains a novelist, as Borges's tale contains Scheherazade within Scheherazade, who wants to write a book that will contain only the pure pleasure of anticipation of the beginning, 'a book that is only an incipit' a book with no ending, perhaps like the Arabian Nights.

Marcel Proust saw himself as Scheherazade, in relation to both sex and death. He describes his Narrator's ingenious excuses for not accompanying Albertine on her little expeditions as an exercise of ingenuity greater than Scheherazade's. Albertine, however, is the one of the pair who is 'insatiable for movement and life'. The narrator remarks gloomily that unfortunately, whilst the 'Persian storyteller' put off her death with her ingenuity, he was hastening his own. And at the end of the almost endless novel, he writes a triumphant meditation on the love of death, the sense of the presence of death, which drives him to create his great and comprehensive book, the book of his life. At one point he even personifies this presence of death as 'le sultan Sheriar' who might or might not put a dawn end to the nocturnal writing of what could not be the *Thousand and One Nights* he had so loved as a child. As a child, 'superstitiously attached to books I loved, as to my loves, I could not without horror imagine a work which would be different'. But he has learned that one can only remake what one loves by renouncing it. 'It will be a book as long as the *Thousand and One Nights*, but quite other.' Malcolm Bowie, in his excellent *Proust Among the Stars*, comments that 'the big book of death-defying stories' with which Proust's novel compares itself is not Boccaccio's *Decameron*, in which death appears as a 'horrifying initial trigger to tale-telling' but the *Nights* 'where stories are life'. 'Narrate or die', for Proust's narrator as for Scheherazade is the imperative. By mere sentences placed end on end, one's sentence is commuted for a while, and the end is postponed.'

The Judaeo-Christian culture is founded on a linear narrative in time. It moves forward from creation through history, to redemption in the Christian case, at one point in time, and looks forward to the promised end, when time and death will cease to be. The great novels of Western culture, from *Don Quixote* to *War and Peace*, from *Moby Dick* to *Dr Faustus*, were constructed in the shadow of the one Book and its story. People are excited by millennial events as images of beginnings and ending. There is a difference between these great, portentous histories and the proliferation of small tales that are handed on, like gifts, like objects for delight and contemplation. Borges' hero in *The Garden of Forking Paths* is told of his Chinese ancestor, a man of letters, who retired to write a book and create a labyrinth, which turned out to be the same thing. He was a philosopher obsessed with 'the abysmal problem of time' whose book never uses the word 'time', because it was the solution to the puzzle he posed. Within this 'incomplete, but not false image of the universe' all times coexist, taking one possible path does not preclude taking another. Storytellers like Calvino and Scheherazade can offer readers and listeners an infinity of *incipits*, an illusion of inexhaustibility. Calvino's imaginary novelist sits and stares at a cartoon of Snoopy, sitting at a typewriter, with the caption 'It was a dark and stormy night . . .', the beginning of a circular shaggy dog story. Both cartoons and soap operas are versions of Scheherazade's tale-telling, worlds in which death and endings are put off indefinitely – and age too, in the case of Charlie Brown. High modernism escaped time with epiphanic visions of timeless moments, imagined infinities which have always seemed to me strained, not in the end offering any counter to fear and death. But the small artifices of elegant, well-made tales, and the vulgar satisfaction of narrative curiosity do stand against death. The romantic novelist Georgette Heyer kept few fan-letters, but I saw two – one from a man who had laughed at one of her comic fops on the trolley going to a life-threatening operation, and one from a Polish woman who had kept her fellow-prisoners alive during the war by reciting, night after night, a Heyer novel she knew by heart.

During the bombardment of Sarajevo in 1994 a group of theatre workers in Amsterdam commissioned tales, from different European writers, to be read aloud, simultaneously, in theatres in Sarajevo itself and all over Europe, every Friday until the fighting ended. This project pitted storytelling against destruction, imaginative life against real death. It may not have saved lives but it was a form of living energy. It looked back to the 1001 Nights and forward to the Millennium. It was called Scheherazade 2001.

Notes

Notes

1 Fathers

The first three essays are expanded texts of the Richard Ellmann memorial lectures given at Emory University, March 1999.

1 Hayden White, *The Content of the Form: Narrative Discourse and Historical Representation* (Johns Hopkins University Press, 1987).
2 Ibid., p.148.
3 Henry Green, *Caught* (1943; reissued by Harvill, 1991).
4 Elizabeth Bowen, *Collected Stories* (Penguin, 1980).
5 First published 1948 (Vintage paperback, 1998).
6 Evelyn Waugh, *The Sword of Honour Trilogy* (1952, 1955, 1961; Penguin 1984).
7 Anthony Powell, *The Valley of Bones* (Penguin, 1964).
8 Anthony Powell, *The Military Philosophers* (1968; Fontana paperback, 1988).
9 Muriel Spark, *The Girls of Slender Means* (1963; Penguin, 1966).
10 Penelope Fitzgerald, *Human Voices* (Collins, 1980).
11 Fredric Jameson, 'Postmodernism and Consumer Society' in *Postmodern Culture*, ed. Hal Foster (Pluto Press, 1985), p.116.
12 Julian Barnes, *Staring at the Sun* (1986; Picador, 1987).
13 La Rochefoucauld, *Maximes*, XXVI.
14 William Golding, *Pincher Martin* (Faber & Faber, 1956).
15 Martin Amis, *Time's Arrow* (1991; Penguin, 1992).

2 Forefathers

1 Sir Walter Scott, *Rob Roy* (1818), ed. with Introduction and Notes by Ian Duncan (Oxford's World Classics, Oxford University Press, 1998).

2   Hayden White, *The Content of the Form: Narrative Discourse and Historical Representation* (Johns Hopkins University Press, 1987), p.33.

3   Simon Schama, *Citizens* (Penguin, 1989).

4   John Fowles, *A Maggot* (1985; Vintage paperback, 1996). Quotation from 'Prologue', pp.5–6.

5   Jeannette Winterson, *The Passion* (1987; Penguin, 1988).

6   Richard Sennett, *The Fall of Public Man* (1977; Faber paperback, 1993), p.9.

7   John Fuller, *Flying to Nowhere* (1983; Vintage paperback, 1992).

8   Peter Ackroyd, *Chatterton* (1987; Penguin, 1993).

9   Peter Ackroyd, *Hawksmoor* (1985; Penguin, 1993).

10   Julian Rathbone, *The Last English King* (1997; Abacus paperback, 1998).

11   Julian Barnes, *A History of the World in 10½ Chapters* (1989; Picador paperback, 1990).

12   Graham Swift, *Waterland* (1983, revised edn; Picador paperback, 1992).

13   White, *The Content of the Form*, p.148, quoting Fredric Jameson's Introduction to *The Political Unconscious* (1981), pp.19–20.

14   François Furet, *Interpreting the French Revolution* (1978), trans. Elborg Forster (Cambridge University Press, 1981), p.25.

15   Ibid.

16   Ibid., p.83.

17   Schama, *Citizens*.

18   Hilary Mantel, *A Place of Greater Safety* (1992; Penguin paperback, 1993), p.29.

19   Roberto Calasso, *The Ruin of Kasch* (1983) trans. William Weaver and Stephen Sartarelli (Harvard University Press, 1994), p.182.

20   Ibid., p.253.

21   Ibid., p.254.

22   Penelope Fitzgerald, *The Blue Flower* (1995; Flamingo paperback, 1996).

23   Quoted in Wm. Arctander O'Brien [sic], *Novalis: Signs of Revolution* (Duke University Press, 1995), p.150.

24   Ibid., p.274.

3   Ancestors

1   *The George Eliot Letters*, ed. Gordon S.Haight, (Yale University Press and Oxford University Press, 1954–5), volume V, p.168.

2   The 'Ilfracombe Journal' (8 May–26 June 1856) reprinted in *George Eliot, Selected Essays, Poems and Other Writings*, ed. A.S. Byatt and Nicholas Warren (Penguin Classics, 1990).

3   Lawrence Norfolk, *The Pope's Rhinoceros* (1996; Vintage paperback, 1998).

4   Graham Swift, *Waterland* (1983; revised edn, Picador paperback, 1992).

5   Julian Barnes, *A History of the World in 10½ Chapters* (1989; Picador paperback, 1990).

6   Thomas Hardy, *A Pair of Blue Eyes*, Chapter XXII.

7   Graham Swift, *Ever After* (Picador, 1992).

8   Hilary Mantel, *A Change of Climate* (Viking, 1994).

9   John Fowles, *The French Lieutenant's Woman* (1969; Vintage paperback, 1996).

10   Sally Shuttleworth, 'Natural History: The Retro-Victorian Novel in *The Third Culture: Literature and Science*, ed. Elinor S. Shaffer in the series European Cultures: Studies in Literature and the Arts (Walter de Gruyter and Co. Berlin, 1997).

11   T.S. Eliot 'The Metaphysical Poets', in *Selected Essays* (Faber & Faber, 1951), p.287.

12   Grahame Greene, 'François Mauriac', in *Collected Essays* (Penguin, 1970), p.91.

13   Gillian Beer, *Darwin's Plots* (Routledge & Kegan Paul, 1983), Chapter 6.

14   Ian McEwan, *Enduring Love* (1997; Vintage paperback, 1998).

15   George Eliot, *Middlemarch*, Book II, Chapter XX.

16   Fowles, *The French Lieutenant's Woman*, Chapter 13.

17   Ian Hacking, *The Taming of Chance* (Cambridge University Press, 1990).

18   Penelope Fitzgerald, *The Gate of Angels* (1990; Flamingo paperback, 1991).

19   Hacking, *The Taming of Chance*, p.147.

4   True Stories and the Facts in Fiction

1   Sigmund Freud, *New Introductory Lectures on Psychoanalysis* (1933 [1932]), Lecture 35, 'The Question of a Weltanschauung' (Pelican Freud Library, 1973), Volume 2, pp.209–10.

2   A year or two ago the *Times Literary Supplement* published a review of a book in which a psychoanalytic critic discovered the hidden presence of the word 'anus' in Coriolanus. I know a school-teacher who addressed a class on the Industrial Revolution and was challenged about her use of the word '*manu*facture', which was 'sexist'.

3   John Cheever, 'MENE, MENE, TEKEL, UPHARSIN' in *The Stories of John Cheever* (Jonathan Cape, 1979).

4   V.S. Naipaul, *The Enigma of Arrival* (Penguin, 1987), p.57–8.

5   'One novel in five hundred or a thousand has the quality a novel should have to make it a novel – the quality of philosophy. I find that I read

with *the same kind of curiosity* most novels, and a book of reportage. Most novels, if they are successful at all, are original in the sense that they report the existence of an area of society, a type of person, not yet admitted to the general literate consciousness.' Doris Lessing, *The Golden Notebook* (Michael Joseph, 1963), p.59.

The Golden Notebook seems to me one of the most far-reaching examinations of the nature of fiction and writing in our time.

I have written about this in an essay, 'People in Paper Houses: Attitudes to "Realism" and "Experiment" in English Post-War Fiction,' reprinted in A.S. Byatt, *Passions of the Mind* (Chatto & Windus, 1991), pp.165 et seq.

6 Lessing, *The Golden Notebook*, pp.98–9.

7 Ibid., pp.402–3.

8 For instance, for Jacobus's analysis of the relations between the metaphor of theatre, the theatrical nature of the events of the French Revolution and Wordsworth's use of this metaphor.

9 Mary Jacobus, *Romanticism, Writing and Sexual Difference: Essays on The Prelude* (Clarendon Press, 1989), p.242.

10 Ibid., p.193.

11 Ibid., pp.263–4.

12 Ibid., Chapter 3, 'Geometric Science and Romantic History or Wordsworth, Newton and the Slave Trade', pp.69 et seq.

13 No longer true in 2000. I have written a short story 'Jael', about an unpleasant and mendacious narrator (which prompted a scornful and hostile letter from a reader who insisted on seeing it as an auto-biographical confession) and a short novel, *The Biographer's Tale*, which is about the relations of biography, autobiography, truth and fiction, and has a male first-person narrator who is a renegade deconstructionist in search of elusive 'things'.

14 The book in question is Michael Meredith (ed.), *More than Friend: The Letters of Robert Browning to Katharine de Kay Bronson* (Armstrong Browning Library of Baylor University and Wedgestone Press, 1985).

15 Quoted in *The Letters of Arthur Henry Hallam*, ed. Jack Kolb (Ohio State University Press, 1981), p.799.

16 Ibid., p.802.

17 Alex Owen, *The Darkened Room: Women, Power and Spiritualism in Late Victorian England* (Virago, 1989).

18 Alfred Tennyson, *In Memoriam A.H.H.*, LXXXIV, in *The Poems of Tennyson*, ed. Christopher Ricks, 2nd edn (Longman, 1987), pp.395–6. All quotations from Tennyson are from this edition.

19 Reprinted in John Kilham (ed.), *Critical Essays on the Poetry of Tennyson* (Routledge, 1960).

20 A.H. Hallam, in *The Writings of Arthur Hallam*, ed. T.H. Vail Motter

(Oxford University Press, 1943), 'Theodicea Novissima', p.204.

21 Hallam, *Letters*, p.423, n.

22 Michael Wheeler, *Death and the Future Life in Victorian Literature and Theology* (Cambridge, 1990). See for instance plates 9, 10, and 11 and pp.148–50. Professor Wheeler's book appeared whilst I was writing *The Conjugial Angel* – I had already talked to him about Swedenborg and spiritualism and *In Memoriam*.

23 Hallam Tennyson, *Alfred Lord Tennyson: A Memoir* (1898), volume I, p.320.

24 2 Corinthians 12: 2–5.

25 Keats to Benjamin Bailey, 22 November 1817: 'O for a Life of Sensations rather than Thoughts! It is a "Vision in the form of Youth" a Shadow of reality to come – and this consideration has further convinced me for it has come as auxiliary to another favorite Speculation of mine, that we shall enjoy ourselves here after by having what we called happiness on Earth repeated in a finer tone and so repeated – '.

26 Hallam, *Letters*, p.509.

27 Emanuel Swedenborg, *Four Leading Doctrines of the New Church* (London, 1846), p.46, section 35.

28 I quote this, which I came across by accident whilst doing a 'trawling' kind of reading for *Angels*, as an example of the way in which happenstance discoveries are made. I had already written most of my text and Sophie was long-since named.

These ideas are closely related to the Gnostic conception of Sophia-Achamoth in Irenaeus. He reports that the [reflection] of the Sophia who dwells above, compelled by necessity, departed with suffering from the Pleroma into the darkness and empty spaces of the void. Separated from the light of the Pleroma, she was without form or figure, like an untimely birth, because she comprehended nothing [i.e. became unconscious]. But the Christ dwelling on high, outstretched upon the cross, took pity on her, and by his power gave her a form, but only in respect of substance, and not so as to convey intelligence [i.e. consciousness]. Having done this, he withdrew his power, and returned [to the Pleroma], leaving Achamoth to herself, in order that she, becoming sensible of the suffering caused by separation from the Pleroma, might be influenced by the desire for better things, while possessing in the meantime a kind of odour of immortality left in her by Christ and the Holy Spirit.' (*Adversus haereses*, I, 4)

According to these Gnostics, it was not the Primordial Man

who was cast out as a bait into the darkness, but the feminine figure of Wisdom, Sophia-Achamoth. In this way the masculine element escaped the danger of being swallowed by the dark powers and remained safe in the pneumatic realm of light, while Sophia, partly by an act of reflection and partly driven by necessity, entered into relation with the outer darkness. The sufferings that befell her took the form of various emotions – sadness, fear, bewilderment, confusion, longing; now she laughed and now she wept. From these affects arose the entire created world.

C.G. Jung, *Alchemical Studies*, trans. R.F.C. Hull (1967; Routledge & Kegan Paul, paperback, 1983), p.334–5.

Gnostic Aeons, according to W.R. Newbold (*Journal of Biblical Literature*, 1912) are the hypostasised thoughts of God, and emanated in pairs, male and female, not unlike the conjugial angels.

29   Hallam, *Writings*, ed. Motter, p.193.
30   Maurice Maeterlinck *La Vie des fourmis* (Bibliothèque-Charpentier, 1930), pp.68–70.

English translation by Bernard Miall, (George Allen & Unwin, 1958), pp.48–50:

Each female has five or six mates, whom she often carries off with her in her flight, and who wait their turn; after which, falling to the ground, they perish in a few hours' time. The fertilized female alights, seeks shelter in the grass, discards her four wings, which fall at her feet like a wedding-gown at the close of the feast, brushes her corselet, and proceeds to excavate the soil in order to cloister herself in an underground chamber, and there attempt to found a new colony.

The foundation of this colony, which frequently ends in disaster, is one of the most pathetic and heroic episodes of insect life.

The ant who will perhaps be the mother of an innumerable population buries herself in the ground and there makes for herself a narrow prison. She has no other food than that which she carries in her body, that is, in the social crop – a little store of honey-dew – her tissues, and her muscles, and above all the powerful muscles of her sacrificed wings, which will be entirely reabsorbed. Nothing enters her tomb save a little moisture, pluvial in origin, and, it may be, certain mysterious effluvia of which we do not as yet know the nature. Patiently she awaits the accomplishment of her secret task. At last a few eggs are spread about her. Presently a larva emerges from one of these eggs; it spins its cocoon; other eggs are added to the first; two or three larvae emerge. Who feeds them? It can only be the mother, since the cell is impervious to everything but a little moisture. Now she has been buried for five or six months; she can do no more, for she is nothing but a skeleton. Then the horrible tragedy begins. On the point of death – a death which would at one blow destroy the future which she has been preparing – she resolves to eat one or two of her eggs, which will give her strength to lay three or four more; or she resigns herself to devouring one of the larvae, which will enable her, thanks to the imponderable aliments whose nature is unknown to us, to rear and nourish two more; and so, from infanticide, to parturition, from parturition to infanticide, taking three steps forward and falling two back, yet steadily gaining on death, the funereal drama unfolds itself for close upon a year, until two or three little workers emerge, weakly because ill-nourished, from the egg, who pierce the walls of the *In Pace*, or rather the *In Dolore*, and seek, in the outer world, their first victuals, which they carry to their mother. From this moment she has no more cares, no more troubles, but night and day, until her death, does nothing but lay her eggs. The heroic days are gone; abundance and prosperity replace the long famine; the prison expands and becomes a city, which spreads underground year after year; and Nature, having here played out one of her cruellest and most inexplicable games, goes farther afield, and repeats the same experiments, whose morality and untility are as yet beyond our understanding.

31 A. Maitland Emmett, *The Scientific Names of the British Lepidoptera: Their History and Meaning* (Harley Books, 1991), pp.16–19.

32 Henry Walter Bates, *The Naturalist on the River Amazon* (1863), Chapter III. The name Eugenia appears in the earlier editions – by the Popular edition of 1910 it is changed to *Morpho Uraneis*.

33 Asa Gray, *Darwiniana*, ed. A. Hunter Dupree (Harvard University Press, 1963), pp.119–20, in an essay entitled 'Natural Selection and Natural Theology', first published in the *Atlantic Monthly* in 1860.

34 Charles Darwin, *The Origin of Species* (Penguin edition, 1968, pp.218–9).
See Gillian Beer's discussion of Darwin's use of metaphor and personification in *Darwin's Plots* (Routledge, 1983). I am also deeply indebted to her discussion of the idea of sexual selection and its use in Victorian fiction, particularly in *Daniel Deronda*.

35 Derek Wragge Morley, *The Evolution of an Insect Society* (Allen &

Unwin, 1954).

36   See note 31.

37   Spenser, *The Faerie Queene* Mutabilitie Cantos, VII. Christopher Ricks refers readers to William Heckford's *Succinct Account of All the Religions* (1791) of which a copy was at Somersby and which describes the statue of Truth at Sais on whose temple was 'the following remarkable inscription: "I am all that hath been, is, and shall be, and my veil hath no mortal yet uncovered."' Tennyson, *Poems*, ed. Ricks, volume II, p.374.

38   I have discussed this at greater length in 'People in Paper Houses', in *Passions of the Mind*.

5   Old Tales, New Forms

Expanded text of the Finzi-Contini lecture given at Yale University, March 1999).

1   Italo Calvino, 'Two Interviews on Science and Literature' (1968), reprinted in *The Literature Machine*, trans. Patrick Creagh (Picador, 1989).

2   Roberto Calasso, *The Marriage of Cadmus and Harmony* (1988) trans. Tim Parks (Jonathan Cape, 1993), pp.10–11.

3   Ibid., pp.136–7.

4   Friedrich Nietzsche, *The Birth of Tragedy*, XXIII, trans. Francis Golffing (Doubleday, 1956).

5   Calasso, *The Marriage of Cadmus and Harmony*, pp.278–9.

6   Ibid., p.22.

7   Italo Calvino, 'Cybernetics and Ghosts', reprinted in *The Literature Machine* (Picador, 1989), p.18.

8   Ibid., p.23.

9   Italo Calvino, *Six Memos for the Next Millennium* (1988) trans. Patrick Creagh (Jonathan Cape, 1992).

10   Calvino, 'Ovid and Universal Contiguity', in *The Literature Machine*, p.151.

11   Doris Lessing, *The Golden Notebook*, (Michael Joseph, 1963) Section 3, The Blue Notebook.

12   Walter Benjamin, 'The Storyteller', in *Illuminations*, trans. Harry Zohn (Fontana paperback, 1973).

13   Malcolm Bowie, *Proust Among the Stars* (HarperCollins, 1998), p.315.

14   Robert Langbaum, *The Gayety of Vision: A Study of Isak Dinesen's Art* (Chatto & Windus, 1964).

15   Karen Blixen (Isak Dinesen), *Seven Gothic Tales* (1934; Penguin paperback, 1963).

16   Gesualdo Bufalino, *Night's Lies*, (1988), trans. Patrick Creagh (Harvill, 1991).

17   Cees Nooteboom, *The Following Story* (1993), trans. Ina Rilke (Harvill, 1994).

18   W.G. Sebald, *The Emigrants* (1993), trans. Michael Hulse (Harvill, 1996).

19   Claudio Magris, *Danube* (1986), trans. Patrick Creagh (Harvill, paperback, 1997).

20   Jorge Luis Borges, *The Garden of Forking Paths* (1941), in *Collected Fictions* trans. Andrew Hurley (Allen Lane, 1999).

21   See the Buenos Aires magazine *Sur* (May–June 1966).

22   See above, note 12.

23   I owe this information to my Danish translator, Claus Bech.

24   Italo Calvino, *If on a Winter's Night a Traveller* (1979), trans. William Weaver (Everyman's Library, 1993).

25   Italo Calvino, *Fiabe Italiane (volume primo)* (1956; Mondadori paperback, 1968).

26   Tzvetan Todorov, *Introduction à la littérature fantastique* (Seuil, 1970).

27   Cees Nooteboom, *In the Dutch Mountains* (1984), trans. Adrienne Dixon (Penguin, 1991).

28   Terry Pratchett, *Witches Abroad* (1991; Corgi paperback, 1992).

6   Ice, Snow, Glass

First published in an anthology called *Mirror, Mirror on the Wall: Women Writers Explore Their Favourite Fairy Tales*, ed., Kate Bernheimer (Anchor Books, 1998).

1   The references to Snow White are from the 3-volume Insel Taschenbuch edition of *Kinder und Hausmärchen gesammelt durch die Brüder Grimm* (1974). Sneewitchen is in volume 1 (112), p.300. The translation is my own.

2   The edition I have used of Hans Andersen is the Bodley Head one of 1935 (reprinted London, 1967). Regrettably no translator is credited.

3   I have taken the story of the princess on the glass mountain from Joanna Cole, *Best-loved Folktales of the World* (Anchor Books, Doubleday, NY), p.78. I have played around with the language of this translation a bit – as a child I always thought of it as a glass *mountain*, not a hill, so I have used both. And I have substituted the Norwegian Askelad for the English 'Boots' which gives a different feel from Ash-Lad. This is not the edition I originally met the story in, but the only one to hand.

4   *The Glass Coffin* (Der gläserne Sarg) is from the same edition of Grimm,

volume 3 (114), p.97. Again the translation is my own, and I have twisted the Black-artist to suit my own purposes – one might well translate 'magician' in most contexts.

5   When I checked this poem, which I had quoted from memory, 'I am fire and ice/I freeze and yet am burned', I found I had got it wrong, in the direction of the essay. It can be found (with modernised spelling) in the Carcanet anthology, *Poetry by English Women Elizabethan to Victorian*, ed. R.E. Pritchard (Manchester University Press, 1990).

6   John Beer, 'Ice and Spring: Coleridge's Imaginative Education', in *Coleridge's Variety*, ed. John Beer (Macmillan, 1974), pp.54 et seq.

7   I have used the Arden edition of *The Winter's Tale* (first published 1963); the Penguin *Complete Poems of Keats* (1973) and the Penguin edition of *Middlemarch* (1965).

7   *The Greatest Story Ever Told*

First published under the title 'Narrate or Die: Why Scheherazade Keeps on Talking', *New York Times Magazine* (18 April 1999).

Text Acknowledgments

The author and publishers would like to thank the following for permission to quote copyright material:

PETER ACKROYD: from *Hawksmoor* (Hamish Hamilton, 1985), © Peter Ackroyd, 1985, reprinted by permission of Penguin Books; MARTIN AMIS: from *Time's Arrow or the Nature of the Offence* (Jonathan Cape, 1991), reprinted by permission of The Random House Archive & Library and the Peters Fraser & Dunlop Group Ltd.; JULIAN BARNES: from *A History of the World in 10½ Chapters* (Jonathan Cape, 1989), reprinted by permission of The Random House Archive & Library and the Peters Fraser & Dunlop Group Ltd., and from *Staring at the Sun* (Picador, 1987), reprinted by permission of Macmillan General Books Ltd; KAREN BLIXEN: from *Seven Gothic Tales* (Penguin, 1963), reprinted by permission of The Rungstedlund Foundation; ELIZABETH BOWEN: from *The Heat of the Day* (Vintage, 1998), © 1949 by Elizabeth Bowen, reprinted by permission of Curtis Brown Ltd., London and Alfred A. Knopf, a Division of Random House Inc.; ANTHONY BURGESS: from *Abba Abba* (Mandarin, 1989), © the Estate of Anthony Burgess, reprinted by permission of Artellus Ltd; ROBERTO CALASSO: from *The Ruins of Kasch*, translated by W. Weaver and S. Sartarelli, (Harvard University Press, 1994), reprinted by permission of Harvard University Press, and from *The Marriage of Cadmus and Harmony*, translated by Tim Parks (Jonathan Cape, 1993), reprinted by permission of Random House Archive & Library; ITALO CALVINO: from *The Literature Machine*,

Text Acknowledgments

Books Ltd. and Henry Holt & Company Inc; CLAUDIO MAGRIS: from *Danube*, translated by Patrick Creagh. First published in 1986 by Garzanti editore, Milan. First published in Great Britain in 1989 by Harvill. Copyright © Garzanti editore s.p.a., 1986. English translation © Harvill and Farrar, Straus & Giroux, 1989, reprinted by permission of The Harvill Press; V.S. NAIPAUL: from *The Enigma of Arrival* (Penguin Books, 1987), © 1987 V.S. Naipaul, reprinted by permission of Gillon Aitken Associates Ltd; CEES NOTEBOOM: from *In the Dutch Mountains*, translated by Adrienne Dixon (Penguin, 1991), reprinted by permission of Gillon Aitken Associates Ltd; LAWRENCE NORFOLK: from *The Pope's Rhinoceros* (Vintage, 1998), reprinted by permission of Random House Archive & Library; ANTHONY POWELL: from *The Valley of Bones* (Heinemann, 1964), reprinted by permission of David Higham Associates; TERRY PRATCHETT: from *Witches Abroad* (Victor Gollancz, 1991), reprinted by permission of The Orion Publishing Group Ltd.; JEANETTE WINTERSON: from *The Passion* (Bloomsbury, 1987), reprinted by permission of Bloomsbury Publishing.

Every effort has been made to trace or contact all copyright holders. The publishers would be pleased to rectify any omissions or errors brought to their notice at the earliest opportunity.

Index